T0168699
HEROBRINE'S
LEGACY

Originally published in French under the title *L'Héritage de Herobrine*. © 2019 by Bragelonne, Paris, France. Illustration by Noëmie Chevalier and Érica Périgaud.

Andrews McMeel Publishing
a division of Andrews McMeel Universal
1130 Walnut Street, Kansas City, Missouri 64106
www.andrewsmcmeel.com

20 21 22 23 24 SDB 10 9 8 7 6 5 4 3 2 1

ISBN: 978-1-5248-6064-6
Library of Congress Control Number: 2020930770

Made by:
King Yip (Dongguan) Printing & Packaging Factory Ltd.
Address and location of manufacturer:
Daning Administrative District, Humen Town
Dongguan Guangdong, China 523930
1st printing—3/30/20

Alain T. Puysségur

GREETINGS, MORTAL.

I am Herobrine, the one and only. Everybody knows and fears me. I have destroyed entire realms and reduced civilizations to ashes. Some claim to have seen me, but none who've ever crossed my path have lived to tell it.

Opening this book, you probably thought you were going to have a good time. Oh, how wrong you were! I have infused these pages with my power, and you are now linked to me! I am looking for an heir, you see. And in order to see if you are worthy of this position, I will test your skills. Apparently you know how to read—that's a good start.

We will review all the areas enabling you to survive in Minecraft: exploration, building, farming, mining, and combat. Needless to say, if you're not up to it, you will pay a high price.

Behold the Endercube, a relic of my own design. It contains my legacy: incredible powers and dark knowledge unfathomable to mere mortals. If you deem yourself worthy, you will have to undergo several trials, from the Overworld to the Nether to the End. With these challenges, you will gain experience and level up in order to break the barriers protecting my legacy.

THE NOOB'S GUIDE

In case you aren't the sharpest pickaxe in the minecart, here's a little explanation to get you started. In order to gain access to my powers, you must answer questions, solve puzzles, and overcome trials split into three levels of difficulty: novice, initiate, and expert.

It is essential to follow that order. By answering questions correctly and finding solutions, you will gain experience and progress to the next level. Only by gaining levels will you be able to access the puzzles of the Endercube.

At the end of each trial, you will need to calculate your progress. I advise you to write down your answers before checking the solutions in the back of this book. For each set of questions, note your correct responses and record the corresponding total of points (, , or per question) in the boxes below:

NOTE YOUR NUMBER OF POINTS HERE

At times you will stumble upon strange and unreadable messages. You will only be able to understand them if you finish all the trials and solve the final puzzle of the Endercube.

I won't bother wishing you good luck—you'll need much more than luck to claim my legacy!

HEROBRINE'S PERSONALITY TEST

To start, I'd like to know what kind of noob I'm dealing with. Even if I intend to test your skills through various games, questions, and riddles, I need a general idea of your personality. Here are different scenarios with several options to choose from. Pick whichever suits you the most. Be careful and follow your instincts!

#1

You have just appeared in a new world. What is your first move?

	I gather a few pieces of wood and try to find a mine where I can quickly get some iron and coal.
	Nightfall is coming soon. I should start building a house right away, even if it's made of dirt and wood.
	I need some equipment, and fast. I try to find some wood to build a pickaxe—then a sword for hunting and defending myself.
	I don't really like this place. I'm sure I could find something nicer.

#2

The sun begins to set, and you haven't had time to build a shelter. What do you do?

	I try looking for high ground: there may be fewer monsters, and I'll get a good look at my surroundings.
	I promptly dig a hole in a mountainside, and then I plug the entrance with some dirt. Hopefully, I will find some coal for a torch.
	I'm sure I can build a small shack with a dozen cubes of wood. Who needs comfort when life is on the line?
	Armed with my magnificent wooden sword, I fear nothing. I will face any danger whatsoever . . . even if it means a little running when the odds aren't in my favor.

#3

You spot another adventurer in your path, but his intentions aren't clear. What do you do?

	I unsheathe my sword, just in case.
	I leave without a word and see how he reacts.
	I try to talk to him. Maybe he has some stuff to trade.
	I invite him over to my place. If I'm friendly to him, surely he'll be friendly to me.

#4

You have just been told that the nearby village has been attacked by a horde of zombies, skeletons, and creepers. What's the best thing to do?

	I try to get materials to them as soon as possible. I know that creepers can cause serious damage.
	I must avenge those poor villagers! I'll track down this horde and put an end to their misdeeds.
	The village must be too exposed. I'll help them find a better location, one easier to defend.
	I really need to teach them how to set traps and dig underground escape tunnels.

#5

During one of your expeditions, you encounter a powerful mage who offers you several sets of items. Which set do you prefer?

⬭	A piece of leather, a map, and a couple of torches.
⬣	A few torches, a chest, and a clock.
◆	A crafting table, a hoe, and a map.
▱	A compass, a crafting table, and a fishing pole.

#6

While coming back home at nightfall, you stumble upon a strange portal that seems to attract more and more monsters. What do you do?

▱	I note the location of this portal so I can return later, at a safer time.
◆	I could get hurt if I step too close. I prefer to stay at a safe distance and study the portal.
⬣	A well-placed block of TNT should put an end to this evil gathering!
⬭	I think it's time to go chop up some mobs and see where this portal leads!

#7

If you had to kiss one monster, which one would it be?

⬣	A creeper. It stings a bit but gives your complexion a healthy glow.
⬭	An enderman. He teleports so fast that I might have a chance to escape afterward.
⬮	A witch. Maybe I'll gain some incredible powers.
⬢	A zombie pigman. It's as if my heart's been struck by lightning!

What do you mean, this question makes no sense? I'll be the judge of that, thank you very much! I'm trying to figure out how twisted you are!

#8

While you were gathering daisies and tulips to decorate your home, you got lost. Here are your choices:

	I could try to find a horse and tame it. I would cover more ground and find my way home faster.
	I need to think logically! I'll leave a trail of wheat seeds behind me to avoid going around in circles.
	I see a giant taiga biome in the distance. By climbing to the top of a tree, I may be able to orient myself and find my way back.
	There's a small hill over there with some stone around it. I'll gather some blocks and build myself a tower to look at my surroundings.

#9

You are facing the ender dragon, the most powerful foe in Minecraft—besides me, of course. What strategy will you use, given you don't know the first thing about dragon slaying?

	A dragon? Oh, I already escaped the End! Like, forever ago.
	I will watch her to understand her moves. I want to know my enemy.
	I'm itching to whack some End crystals, just to see what happens. Who knows, maybe they have something to do with this big old mob?
	In order to fight her, I need to understand my surroundings. I'll try a stealthy approach.

#10

You have accomplished most of your objectives, vanquished countless enemies, and constructed dozens of buildings. What will you do now?

	Start all over elsewhere!
	A kingdom is never finished. Mine will keep expanding forever!
	Now that I rule the Overworld, I need to conquer what lies beneath it.
	There will always be people to protect. And I'm ready!

RESULTS

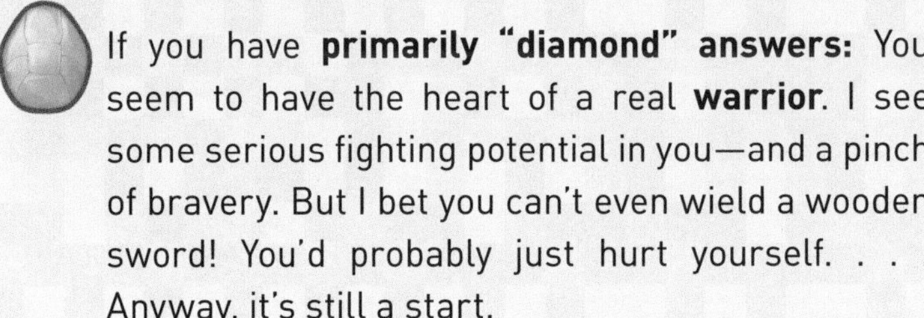

If you have **primarily "diamond" answers:** You seem to have the heart of a real **warrior**. I see some serious fighting potential in you—and a pinch of bravery. But I bet you can't even wield a wooden sword! You'd probably just hurt yourself. . . . Anyway, it's still a start.

If you have **primarily "redstone" answers:** So you have the heart of a **builder**, huh? Well, it takes all types. Personally, I'd rather destroy buildings than create them. In any case, don't get too excited! Just because you can stack two blocks of dirt doesn't mean creating an entire kingdom will be a cinch.

If you have **primarily "emerald" answers:** Well, the heart of a **miner** it is. You seem particularly attracted to shiny materials and dark underground passageways. This means you'll need a perfect sense of direction, not to mention serious guts. And you'd better learn how to swing a pickaxe and use TNT without blowing yourself up!

If you have **primarily "gold" answers:** Do you dream of faraway lands and lost countries? This means you've got the heart of an **explorer**. That's not to say you won't get lost, but at least you're not afraid—or not too afraid. I'm guessing it's because you have no idea what's waiting for you out there. . . .

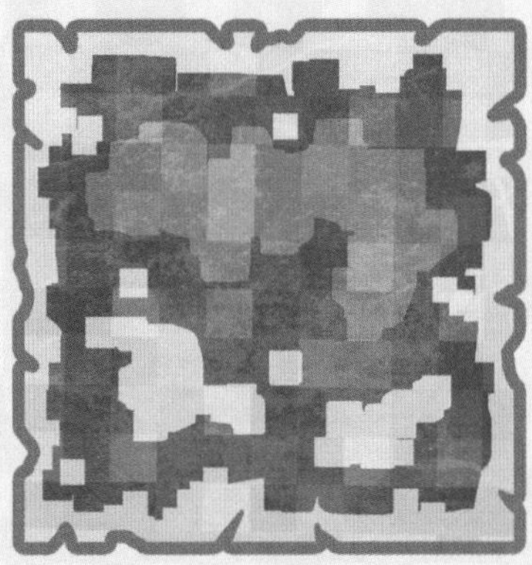

NOVICE

THE EXPLORATION TRIAL

Long before I acquired my current power, I was already thirsty for knowledge and adventure. I was able to survive in any kind of environment imaginable before you were even born. Now I want to know if you are a worthy explorer. You'll need unmatched orientation skills and eyes as sharp and bright as mine! It would be such a pain if you got lost and devoured at nightfall during one of my trials. Not that I would cry over it—I hate wasting my time! Let's start easy by roaming the Overworld.

Minecraft is a vast world filled with numerous biomes to explore and natural wonders to discover. In the list below, which of these biomes doesn't exist?

1. Desert.
2. Plains.
3. Taiga.
4. Volcano.
5. Swamp.

Given your undoubtedly limited memory, I strongly suggest you map your surroundings. In the crafting table below, what element is missing to create your map?

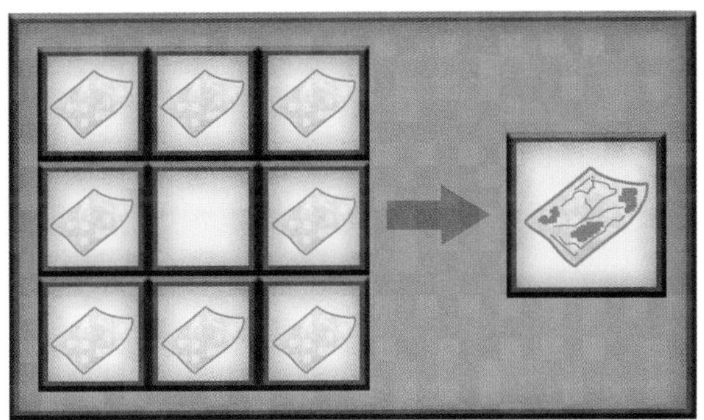

NOTE YOUR NUMBER OF POINTS HERE

Sometimes boats will be your only option for efficiently reaching faraway islands or sunken temples. How many people can a boat hold?

1. One.
2. Two.
3. Three.

#4 

Before building something—a stone tower, for instance—to get a better vantage and find your way around, you'd better identify some natural landmarks first. In this image, which element will make it easy to get your bearings?

#5

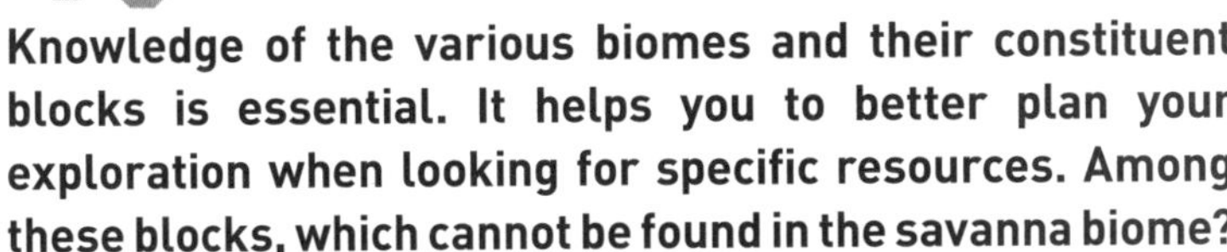

Knowledge of the various biomes and their constituent blocks is essential. It helps you to better plan your exploration when looking for specific resources. Among these blocks, which cannot be found in the savanna biome?

   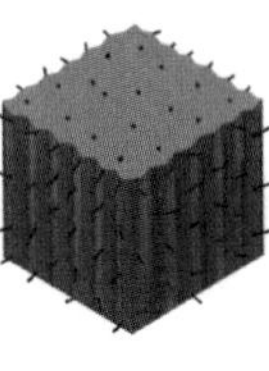 

NOTE YOUR NUMBER OF POINTS HERE

If you've managed to get here, you may just have a chance. At least you know the basics. . . . But don't get too excited just yet—a blind sheep could've made it this far!

#6   

Any self-respecting explorer is both cautious and attentive. Only then can you spot the resources around you. Can you tell me which of these blocks doesn't have an identical match?

#7

There are some strange and mystical places in Minecraft, like these temples. Where can you find them?

1. In the jungle.
2. In the taiga.
3. In the forest.
4. In the Nether.
5. In the End.

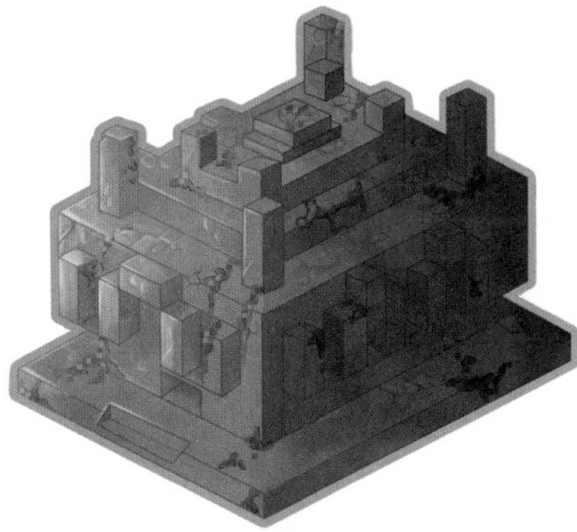

Can't decipher this? If you make it to the end of my trials, you'll discover the key.

Sometimes, you need to move faster. Rank these means of transportation from the fastest to the slowest.

1. A boat.
2. A pig.
3. A horse.

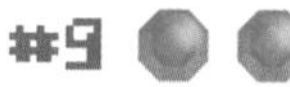

Exploring is one thing, but you shouldn't go out on an adventure without checking the weather forecast. The sun and the moon are valuable signs, but can you see them when it rains in Minecraft?

#10

During an excursion, you have to be very attentive to the animals around you. While some are just waiting passively for you to cut them up and eat them, others are much less friendly. Polar bears, for instance, are dangerous creatures. When are they likely to attack?

1. At any moment—these are hostile monsters.
2. If you wander too close to their cubs.
3. Never, unless you attack them first.

You don't know the answer to that question? I hope you can run fast, since it looks like you'll need to. . . .

NOTE YOUR NUMBER OF POINTS HERE

Assuming you are a noob—which is a safe bet in your case—what is the best way to react when, while exploring a swamp, you come across a witch hut?

1. Hightail it outta there!
2. Go check it out.
3. Set the nearby trees on fire.

I've met many witches in my time, but none of them as devious as the one called Glitchwitch. She had incredible powers and extraordinary knowledge. With a single glance, she would have seen your inner weaknesses and annihilated you in the blink of an eye. I learned much from her fortitude.

Holy creeper! If there's one thing that bugs me, it's the villagers and their annoying voices! "Hrrrrg! Hrrrrg!" The only upside is that it's easy to tell them apart and destroy them in the proper order. What is the profession of a villager clad in white?

1. Priest.
2. Librarian.
3. Farmer.

#13

My legacy isn't meant for just anyone. You need to demonstrate your reasoning. For this, I've come up with a little role-playing exercise: on the map here, find the right path to get to the chest without starving to death. You may move in any direction except diagonally, and you need to eat at least one apple every three moves.

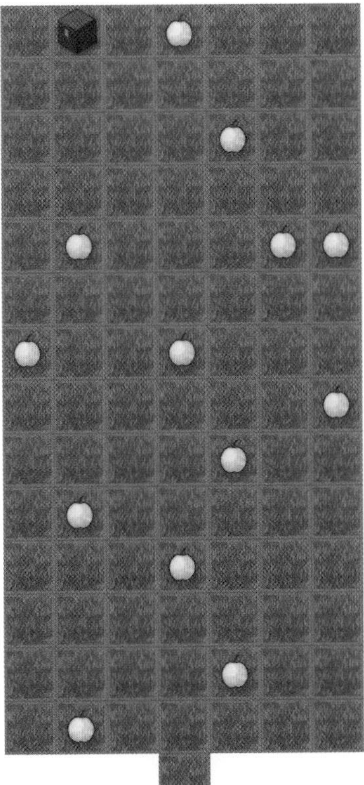

NOTE YOUR NUMBER OF POINTS HERE

#14 

Sometimes you find surprising things deep in the oceans, like underwater monuments. But how can you reach them without drowning? As I suspect you're not yet able to brew a water-breathing potion, what primitive survival method could you use to breathe underwater?

1. Surrounding yourself with blocks of glass.
2. Placing a torch underwater on the block in front of you.
3. Putting a pumpkin on your head.

#15

Are you ready to be scarred forever? No? Well that's too bad, since you'll be visiting the Nether during the next exploration trial! But you'll need to activate the portal first. Among the methods below, which one would work?

1. Make a creeper explode near the portal.
2. Place a redstone torch on the portal.
3. Hold a blaze rod in your hand.

NOTE YOUR NUMBER OF POINTS HERE

You have reached the end of the very first trial. You still have a long and painful way ahead of you. If you don't think you can keep up, go train in Minecraft and come back when you're ready. I don't have time for noobs.

It is now time to judge your progress. You need to reach level 1. Have you gathered enough experience?

Your number of points: ☐

In order to proceed to the building trial, you need at least:

15 points.

If that's not the case, I recommend you train a bit more before proceeding to the next challenge.

THE BUILDING TRIAL

Are you proud of all the experience you've earned? I'll stop you right here: it's far from enough. A llama could get the same results. Besides proving you're worthy of my secrets, don't forget that you must also decipher the puzzles of the Endercube—an impossible task unless you reach the necessary level.

People know me more for destroying than building. But I'm also a great architect. Through cunning and perseverance, I've managed to gain access to the Source Code, the origin of all things in Minecraft. It lets me easily construct the most complex and magnificent buildings. And how about you? If you wish to proceed, you must prove you can do more than just stack blocks of dirt.

Some people—like me—prefer to be alone. That might not be the case for you. If you want to invite villagers to your area until it echoes with their unbearable mumbling, what condition must your village meet?

1. All houses need a wooden door.
2. The village must be protected by a wall to keep night monsters away.
3. There must be chests full of food in the village.

#2

You can quickly find yourself with an inventory full of useless junk, like dozens of cobblestone blocks. Sometimes, you need to sort it out and throw some stuff away. In the list below, which block can be used to dispose of trash?

1. A cactus.
2. A mob spawner.
3. A dragon's head.

I mentioned a dragon's head, but I doubt you would even know where to find one—much less defeat it. That's a point we'll address in the final trials, if you survive until then.

NOTE YOUR NUMBER OF POINTS HERE

#3

It's quite gratifying to gaze upon your armor, dented by many victorious battles. Armor stands are useful for these moments of reflection. What necessary element is missing from the crafting table below?

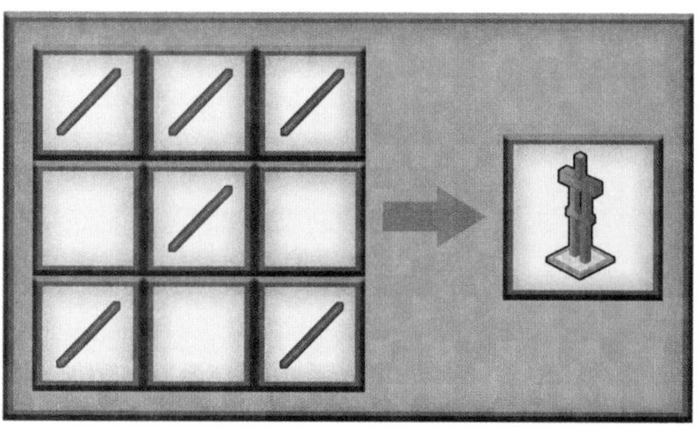

#4

To bring about your architectural ambitions, you'd better warm up that furnace of yours. Rank the fuels below, starting with the one that will keep your furnace burning the longest.

1. A bucket of lava.
2. Some coal.
3. Some planks.
4. A blaze rod.

#5

Redstone is an essential tool in Minecraft, enabling you to automate tasks like farming or to build advanced defense systems. Even redstone novices know the repeater is one of the most useful elements. Why?

1. It accelerates redstone signals.
2. It carries redstone signals beyond fifteen blocks.
3. It generates a direct electrical current.

NOTE YOUR NUMBER OF POINTS HERE

I think you're ready for a new test. I want to know if you can think clearly in stressful situations. Night is falling, and you don't have much time before monsters start to spawn and hunt you. You decide to build a makeshift base. What can you build with this inventory?

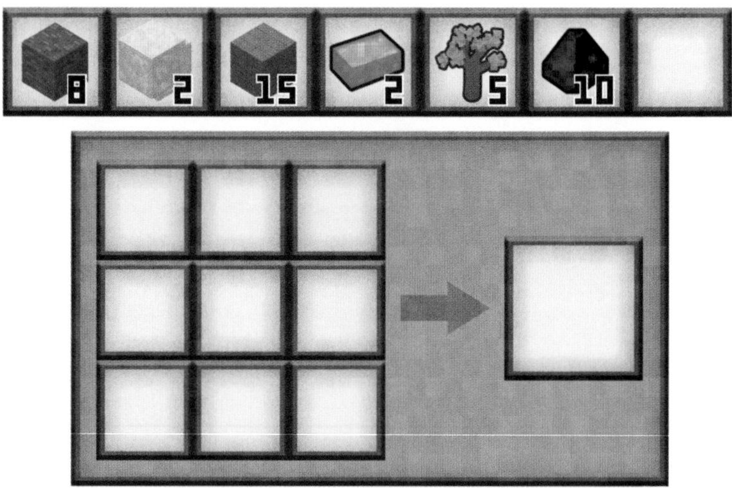

1. One furnace, one crafting table, and one chest.
2. One furnace, one bed, and one shovel.
3. One crafting table, seven torches, and two chests.

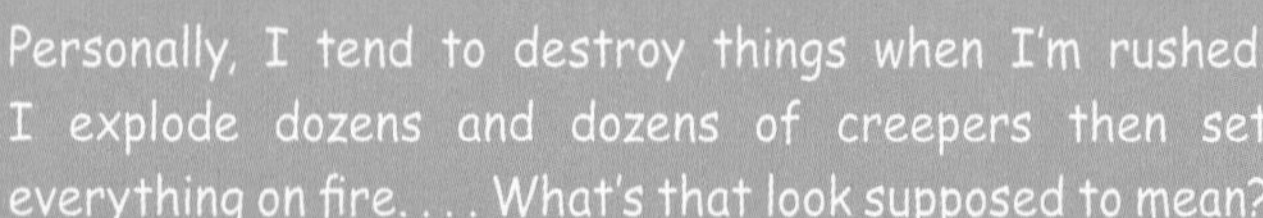

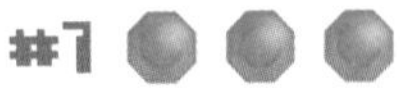

Let's see if you can find these essential crafting elements. . . .

Horizontal

1. I make it possible to see and stay safe.

3. I am almost a demigod.

5. Thanks to me, you are safe in your house.

7. I am essential for creating blocks and items.

Vertical

2. You'll have a hard time digging without me.

4. You'll need me in the darkness.

6. I am used to access basements.

8. BOOOOM!

NOTE YOUR NUMBER OF POINTS HERE

#8

For people of your kind, snow golems are very useful in defense. A crucial element is missing from the snow golem setup below. What is it?

This golem's name is Snowkin. He has been one of my servants for a very long time. You should know that golems are helpful, but not foolproof. I've already paid the price for Snowkin's weaknesses, and since then he has been imprisoned in this tower.

#9 

Feeble beings such as you enjoy creating dirt roads with a shovel. But do you know what purpose they serve?

1. To protect from monsters, since they can't spawn on roads.
2. To walk faster around buildings.
3. To direct traffic for intelligent mobs like villagers and golems.

#10  

If you wish to create truly attractive buildings—which I strongly discourage you from doing for now, given your skill level—you need to be able to produce some light. Can you rank these objects from the brightest to the dimmest?

1. A torch.
2. A burning furnace.
3. A redstone torch.
4. A glowstone.

NOTE YOUR NUMBER OF POINTS HERE

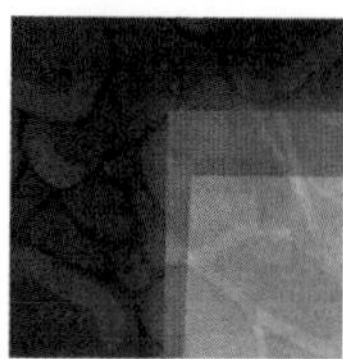

#11  

In the Nether only can I be found.

Light I help detect.

What am I?

#12

Given that Minecraft's monsters can be relentless, this peculiar arrangement can be quite useful. Why?

1. It prevents spiders from going over walls.
2. It can deter slimes.
3. It blocks arrows shot by skeletons below.

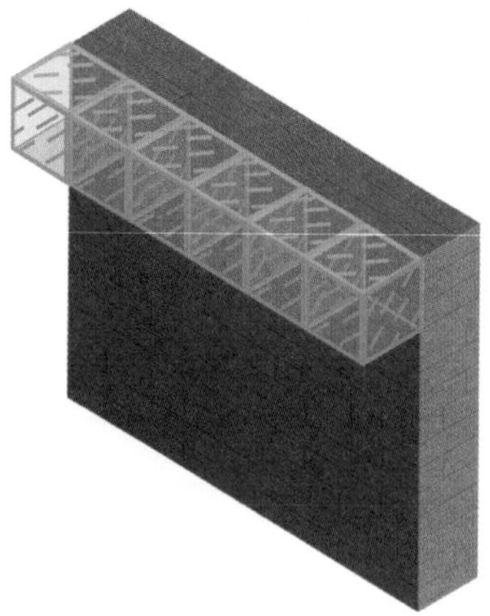

One thing's for sure, this kind of primitive defense wouldn't stop me.

#13

Even though I can devise huge and complex buildings, I won't ask you to do the same. But I still need someone with an eye for detail. Take a look at the house below, and find the corresponding layout.

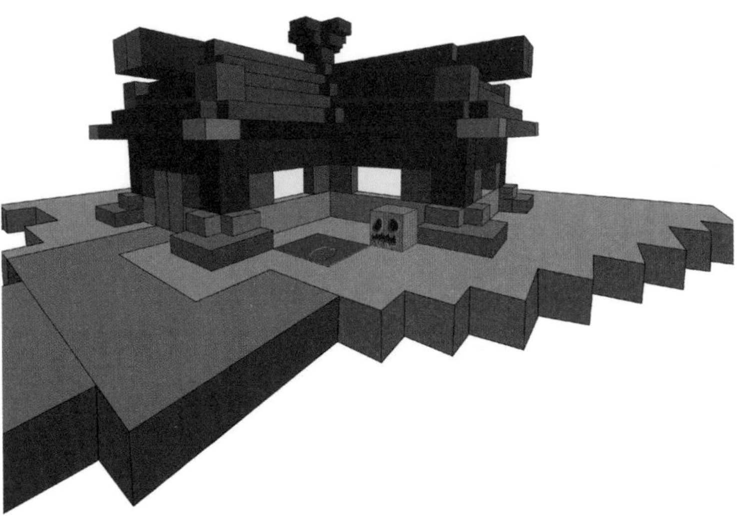

1

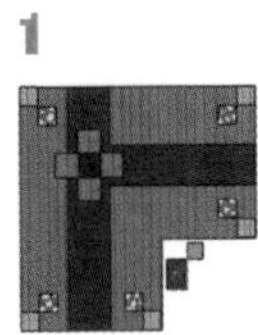

2

3

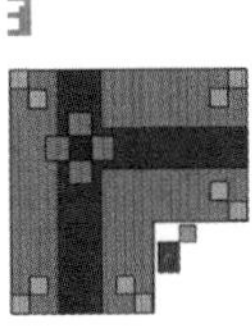

4

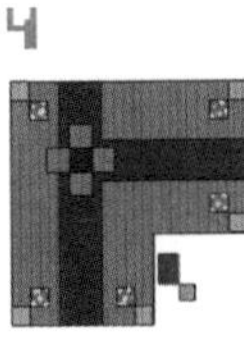

NOTE YOUR NUMBER OF POINTS HERE

There are many kinds of resources in Minecraft, and most of them are essential for building. Take wood, for example: I bet at least one of your projects will be based on that material. Do you know how many types of wood there are in Minecraft?

1. Three: spruce, jungle wood, and dark oak.
2. Four: spruce, jungle wood, birch, and oak.
3. Six: spruce, jungle wood, birch, oak, acacia, and dark oak.

You're not a lost cause! If you don't make it through my trials, at least you can still become a lumberjack. . . .

#15

Part of my strength lies in my ability to analyze and anticipate. I expect the same from you. Can you tell me the logical order of crafting of these elements?

1. A wooden pickaxe.
2. A wooden axe.
3. A furnace.
4. A crafting table.
5. An iron pickaxe.
6. An enchanting table.

You won't survive for long if your buildings can't resist the nightly monster attacks. Believe me, I've been there before. You don't want to see your wooden shack engulfed in flames, smack dab in the middle of a field ravaged by creepers.

But for now, maybe you'll manage to move on to level 2?

Your number of points is:

In order to go on to the farming trial, you need a minimum of:

35 points.

If you have several wrong answers, I hope you'll continue training. I don't like weakness. In fact, I despise it.

THE FARMING TRIAL

You seem to know how to make some basic buildings. That's a start. At least you can protect yourself and prepare for survival. Of course, you are still far from my level of expertise. And to be honest, you'll never reach it. At best you could help me build a soggy dungeon—so I'll have somewhere to put you if you turn out to be an even bigger noob than I thought. And now, if you don't want to starve to death, you should start growing crops and raising livestock. Do you have a green thumb? If the answer is yes, be careful . . . you might be a zombie.

#1

Farming starts with water. Without it, you can't grow much. You must therefore understand how water can irrigate the blocks around it. In the plan below, which dirt blocks are being irrigated?

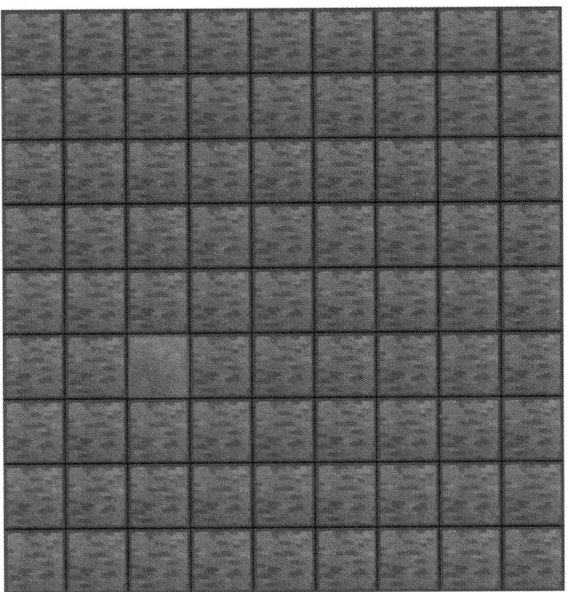

This is basic stuff. If you don't know the answer, I might take you for a little swim. . . .

NOTE YOUR NUMBER OF POINTS HERE

#2 

There are many different plants in Minecraft. In the list below, which do not exist?

1. Melon.
2. Beetroot.
3. Wheat.
4. Corn.
5. Pumpkin.
6. Pear.
7. Carrot.
8. Strawberry.

#3   

To keep trips to a minimum, you should create a source of water near your crops. You have two buckets of water. Where should you pour them to create an infinite source of water?

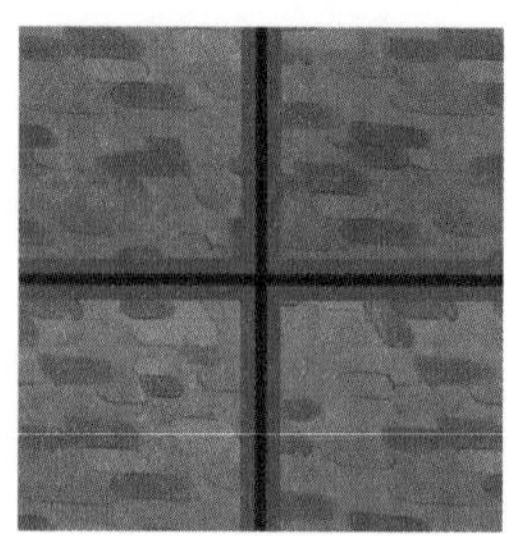

#4

When getting into farming, don't forget about animals. Domesticating peaceful creatures can be a good way to get resources. You still need to place them in an enclosure, however, or they'll keep running away! Do you know what is missing from the crafting table below to create a leash?

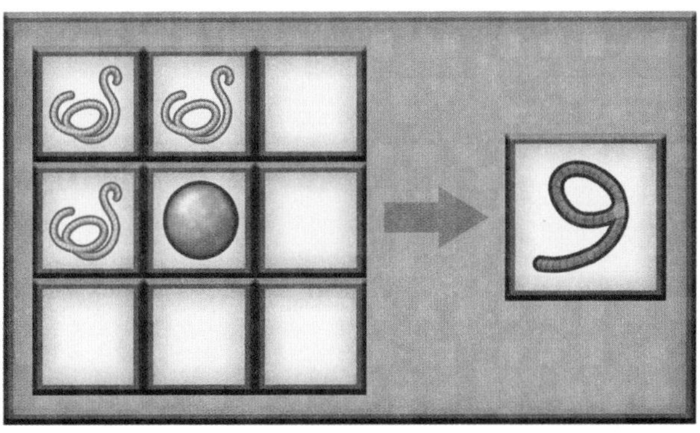

NOTE YOUR NUMBER OF POINTS HERE

#5

Can you pair each animal with its favorite food?

1. Cow.
2. Pig.
3. Rabbit.
4. Chicken.

A. Carrot.
B. Wheat.
C. Dandelion.
D. Pumpkin seed.

Try holding some in your hand and approaching animals to see their reactions. . . .

#6 

As you surely know, beetroot exists in Minecraft. But where exactly can you find it?

1. In villages.
2. In chests found in abandoned mineshafts.
3. In the forest.

Seriously, who eats this stuff? I guess if your only other choice is rotten flesh. . . .

#7  

Speaking of which, let's say that you've just eaten some rotten flesh and poisoned yourself. What do you take to get better?

1. A cookie.
2. A bucket of milk.
3. A pumpkin pie.

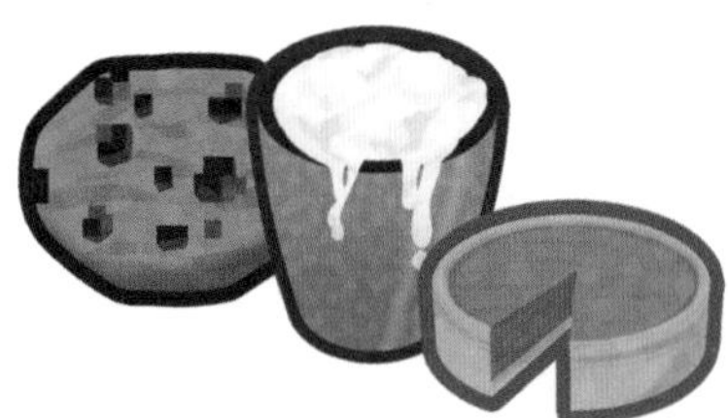

NOTE YOUR NUMBER OF POINTS HERE

What is the maximum number of pumpkins that can grow on this plot of land? Don't forget that they need two blocks to ripen.

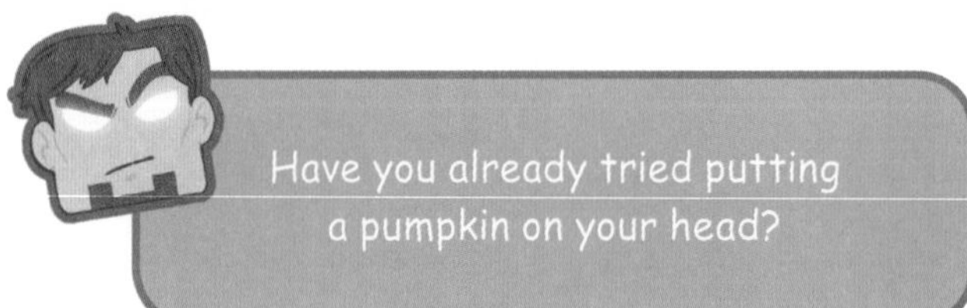

#9 

The llama is certainly a funny creature, but it can also be useful. How many llamas can follow another llama on leash?

1. Seven llamas.
2. Nine llamas.
3. Twelve llamas.

#10

Not only do plants make nice decorations, but they are also essential for coloring objects. Which of these plants yields magenta dye?

1. Lilac.
2. Poppy.
3. Cornflower.
4. Allium.
5. Azure bluet.

NOTE YOUR NUMBER OF POINTS HERE

#11 

What makes it possible (along with a bit of luck) to transform a basic mushroom into a giant mushroom?

1. Water.
2. Bone meal.
3. Tilled soil.
4. Light.

That old crone Glitchwitch loved setting those giant mushrooms on fire and watching the flames spread. She sure knew how to have fun! I bet you've already done it too, right? There's nothing to be ashamed of! My reputation for destruction is well deserved, ha ha ha!

#12 

How can you harvest the maximum number of slices from a melon?

1. With a pickaxe.
2. With an axe.
3. By hand.

#13

Take a good look at these sugar cane plans. Among them is an imposter. Can you find out which one?

NOTE YOUR NUMBER OF POINTS HERE

Silviculture—growing trees—is an essential skill. To ensure that a sapling grows well, how many free blocks in height are needed?

1. Three blocks.
2. Four blocks.
3. Six blocks.

#15

Sometimes, instead of mindlessly killing every creature that moves, you might get the strange idea to feed them. If you feed wheat seeds to a chicken, then feed a second chicken, what might happen?

1. They are going to follow me awhile.
2. They'll fall in love with each other.
3. They'll stop moving for a while.
4. They'll immediately start laying eggs.

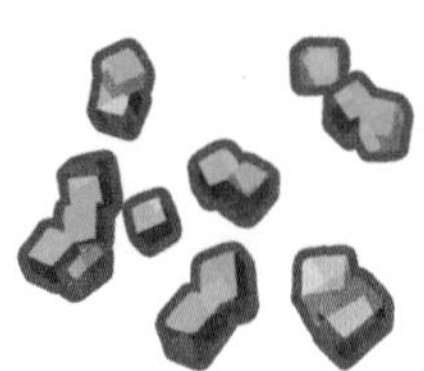

NOTE YOUR NUMBER OF POINTS HERE

Apparently you can feed yourself. You might get food poisoning, but at least you won't kick the bucket. Personally, I no longer require any kind of sustenance since traveling to the End, but that's a story for another time. Of course sometimes I eat when I'm feeling nostalgic—or for the simple pleasure of stealing an innocent creature's meal.

The knowledge you've demonstrated so far is essential. You're not giving up as fast as I thought you would. I'm intrigued, but you're still far from opening the Endercube.

You must now progress to level 3. Do you have the required experience points?

Your number of points is:

In order to proceed to the mining trial, you require at least:

55 points.

THE MINING TRIAL

So you think you're doing fine and the levels are speeding by? Sorry to disappoint, but I simplified your tasks for a good reason: I wanted to build up your confidence. This way you'll be even more disappointed when you fail to solve a riddle in the coming trials. Oh, you think it's cruel? Come on, did you expect me to behave like a nice, tame wolf? You clearly forgot who you are dealing with. . . .

Anyway, it's time for the mining trial, an essential part of, you know, MINEcraft. You will need to become a certified pickaxe master. Can you sense the diamond veins under your feet? I do. It's as if they were part of me!

#1

Can you find the unenchanted diamond pickaxe in this jumble of tools?

NOTE YOUR NUMBER OF POINTS HERE

#2

After many hours of searching, some creeper explosions, and several painful deaths, you stumble upon a vein of diamond ore. Which tool will you use to mine it as quickly as possible?

1. An iron pickaxe.
2. TNT.
3. A gold pickaxe.

#3

Among the following blocks, which one is the strongest?

1. Bedrock.
2. Obsidian.
3. Diorite.
4. Cobblestone.

#4

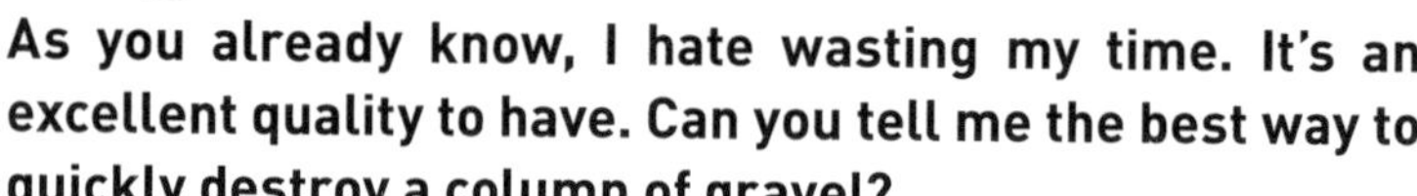

As you already know, I hate wasting my time. It's an excellent quality to have. Can you tell me the best way to quickly destroy a column of gravel?

1. Put some lava on top of it to make it melt.
2. Put a torch at the base of the column, under the first block.
3. Ignite a block of obsidian at the base to consume the whole column.

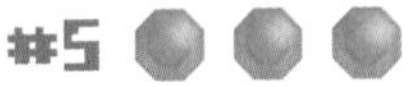

Some pickaxes are already organized below. Can you correctly place the remaining tools?

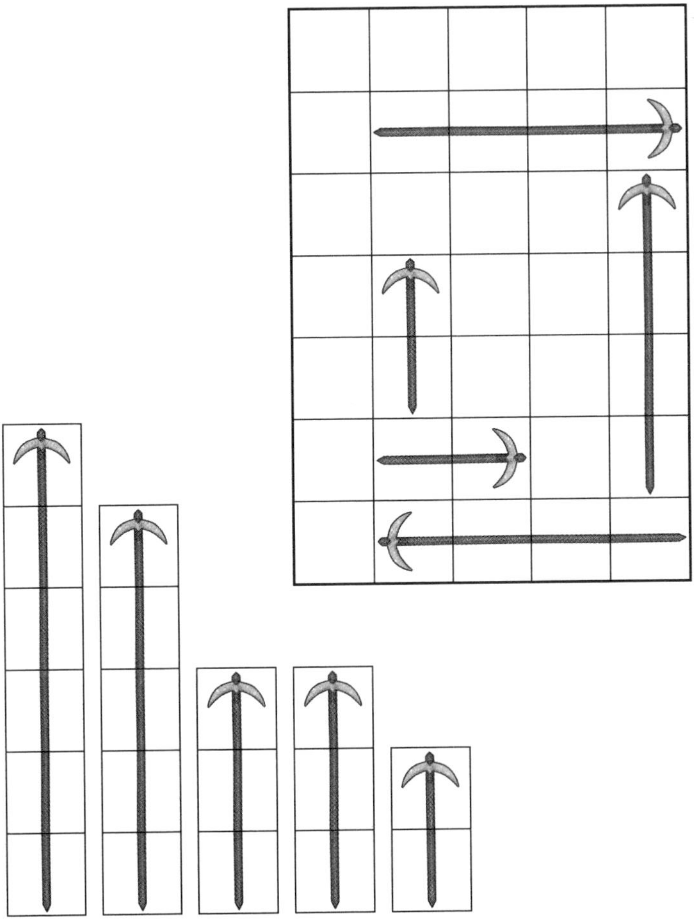

NOTE YOUR NUMBER OF POINTS HERE

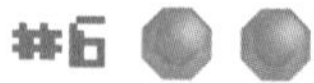

If you decide to go diamond hunting, you'll need to know what's below your feet. Which blocks will you never find if you go mining in the Overworld?

1. A dirt block.
2. A pumpkin block.
3. A cobblestone block.
4. A lava block.
5. An iron block.
6. An ice block.
7. A lapis lazuli block.
8. A soul sand block.
9. A diamond block.
10. A water block.

I already mentioned it, but perhaps you don't know what the Source is? It's the reason Minecraft exists, that creatures live in it, and that lava can burn wood and flesh. Only the Master Crafters can access it. It is both wonderful and terrifying.

Handling the Source Code isn't for just anyone. I am the only one who's been able to access it without being taught by a Master Crafter. That's how I know the position of any block at any moment, allowing me to devise the most terrible plans!

Have you ever stumbled upon a vein of lapis lazuli and shouted with joy before realizing it wasn't diamond? Well, lapis lazuli can still be useful. What for?

1. To dye wood in blue.
2. To dye terracotta in blue.
3. To dye sandstone in blue.

#8

Different types of ore have different spawn rates and rarity. In the list below, do you know which one is even rarer than diamond?

1. Gold.
2. Emerald.
3. Redstone.

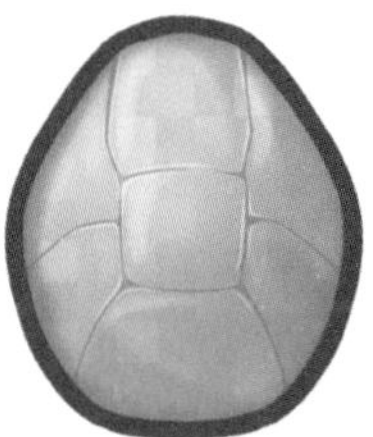

You'll need to become a mineral homing device if you want to craft the finest equipment!

NOTE YOUR NUMBER OF POINTS HERE

I really love abandoned mineshafts. What wonderful places of desolation and melancholy, filled with the lingering scent of exploded creepers! Which of the following can be found in these places?

(Several answers are possible.)

1. Chests.
2. Cave spider spawners.
3. Redstone torches.
4. TNT minecarts.

#10

See that crafting table below? There's something missing that's needed to create rails—what is it?

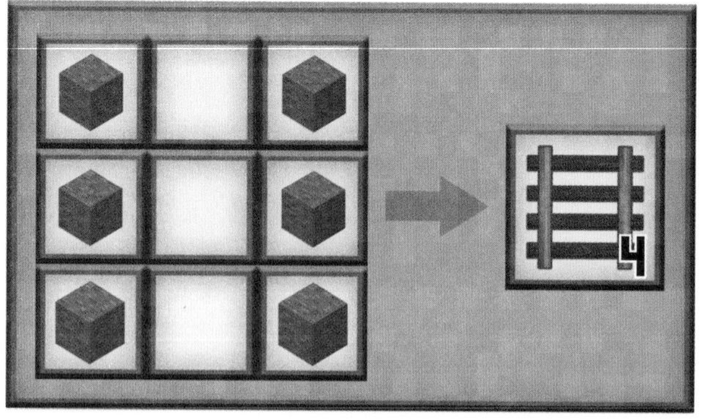

As you lack the gift of teleportation (unlike me), I hope you'll have the sense to use rails. That is, unless you like hiking. . . .

#11 

Redstone powder is essential for numerous crafting recipes. You can get some by mining, but there are other ways to acquire it. Which of the following is one such method?

1. Killing a witch.
2. Killing a villager.
3. Cooking a block of glowstone.

NOTE YOUR NUMBER OF POINTS HERE

If you go mining, you have to watch your stamina. Jumping from block to block can be exhausting, but climbing stairs is less tiring. How many stairs can you craft with these ingredients?

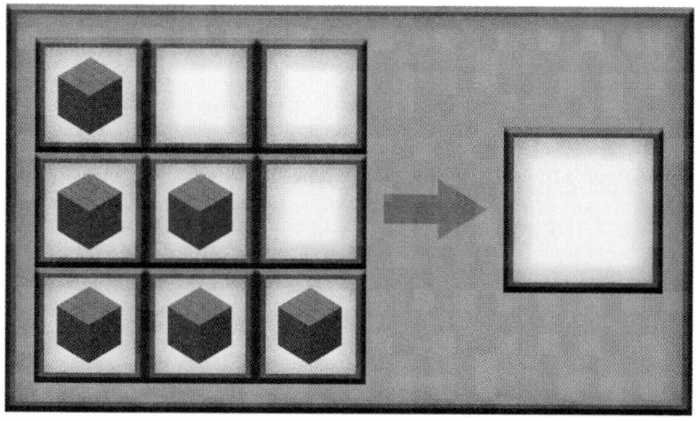

#13

Seeing as we mentioned rails, surely you know there are different types of minecarts. There's one to haul you around, obviously, but there are also others with specific purposes. Which one of these minecarts does not exist?

1. A minecart with hopper.
2. A minecart with glowstone.
3. A minecart with TNT.

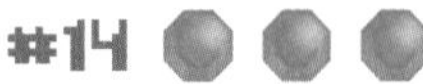

It's very easy to get lost in a mineshaft. In the event you start digging around for diamond ore—or anything else, for that matter—the tunnels will soon become a complicated maze. Prove that you have a natural sense of direction by finding the way out of this labyrinth.

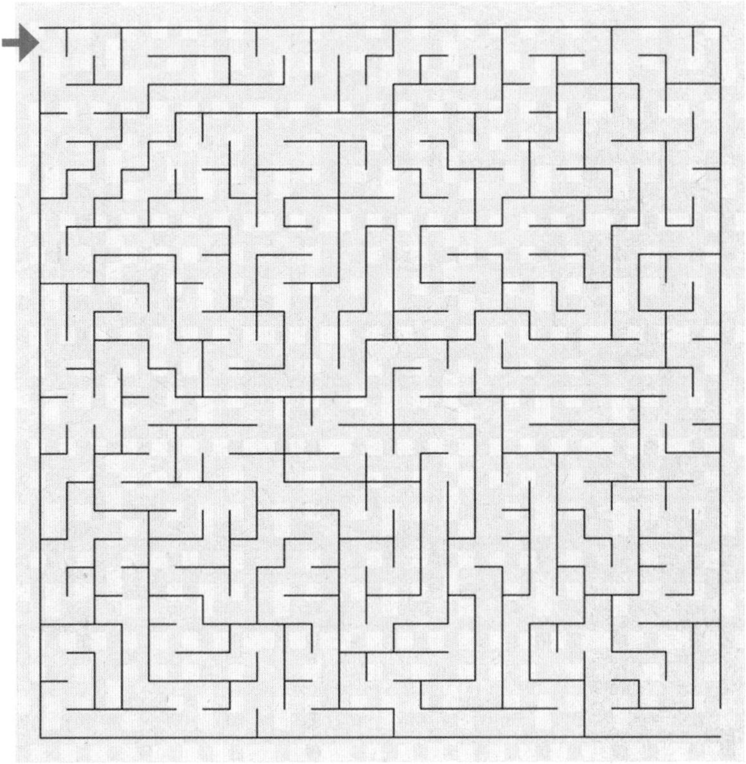

NOTE YOUR NUMBER OF POINTS HERE

Having an organized and calculating mind is a real asset. What can you craft with the following inventory?

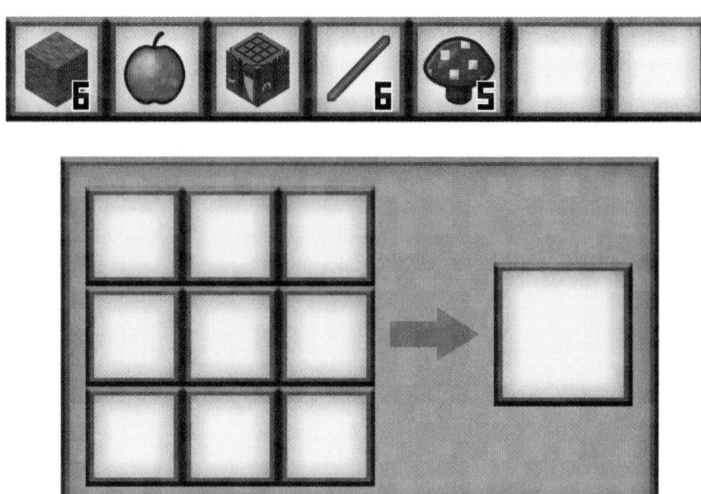

1. One pickaxe, one sword, and two shovels.
2. Two pickaxes and two swords.
3. Two shovels and two swords.

NOTE YOUR NUMBER OF POINTS HERE

Are you ready to continue? There's only one step left before you can tackle the first Endercube puzzle. You're going to need all your mental abilities and all your energy. So I hope the following combat trial will be a mere formality. I also hope that you've gathered enough experience points. To reach level 4, you need at least 80.

Your number of points is:

In order to proceed to the combat trial, you need a minimum of:

80 points.

THE COMBAT TRIAL

I've fought battles more epic than the greatest heroes could ever dream of. Thanks to my fighting skills, I am the best warrior of the three known realms of Minecraft. With my tremendous powers, I can annihilate entire armies in seconds. So I strongly advise you against trying to steal my Endercube. That would be the most foolish idea of all the foolish ideas you've had throughout your foolish existence.

Come on, noob, draw your wooden sword—if you even have one—and let's see what you're worth in battle!

I won't bother asking if you know how to craft a sword. On the other hand, do you know how to make a shield? Something is missing from this crafting table. What is it?

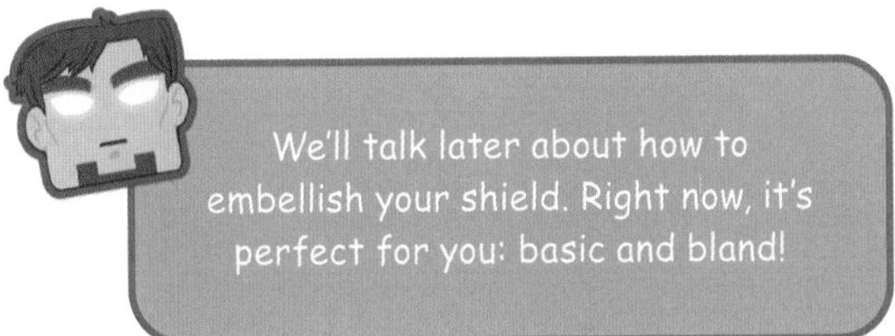

NOTE YOUR NUMBER OF POINTS HERE

#2

Not all Minecraft creatures are as friendly as I am. Most have only one goal: to kill you. In the following list, there are monsters you can't find in the Overworld. Which are they?

1. A creeper.
2. A zombie pigman.
3. A ghast.
4. A baby zombie.
5. An enderman.
6. An evoker.

#3

As you fight, your weapons will wear out and require some maintenance. Do you know how to a perform a unit repair?

1. Take two identical weapons and merge them.
2. Take the damaged weapon and a piece of the same material and merge them.
3. Consume experience to "decraft" the weapon and "recraft" it entirely.

Take a good look at this group of zombies. They're not all identical: one of them doesn't have a duplicate. Can you find it?

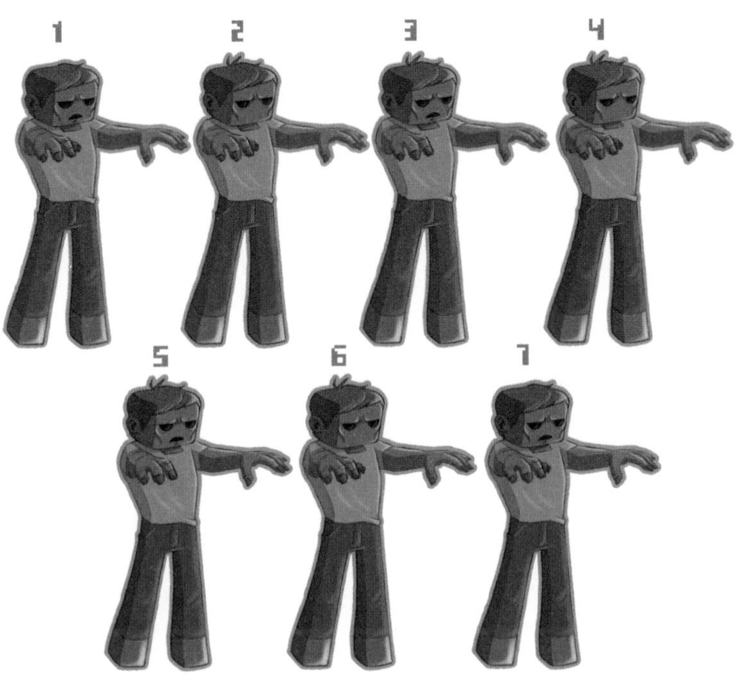

Just like snow golems, zombies aren't exactly known for their intelligence. It's an advantage for people like you, who fight them, but a flaw for people like me, who control them during battles.

#5

Creepers are among the most famous monsters of Minecraft, undoubtedly because players are so afraid of them. They were created in a very special way by Notch, the developer of the Source. Do you know how?

1. Notch used a failed pig model to create creepers.
2. Notch got his inspiration from the failure of an automatically generated biome.
3. Notch merged two hostile monsters that were supposed to be separate entities at first.

#6

Endermen are incredible monsters. No need to go to the End to see them, since some of them spawn after dark. What is their greatest weakness?

1. Fire and lightning.
2. Water and rain.
3. Snowflakes and ice.

Did you know that the Endercube was made with numerous ender pearls? It was no easy feat to get them from endermen, given that they kept teleporting away. If you listen carefully, you can actually hear their voices echoing within the cube. Now endermen can feel the presence of the cube from hundreds of blocks away. They are attracted by its power, but they will never dare approach as long as I'm nearby.

#7

The sun is useful for finding your bearings (and burning many enemies). Unfortunately, not all monsters catch fire during the day. Which ones are safe from sunlight?

1. Zombies.
2. Creepers.
3. Spiders.
4. Skeletons.
5. Slimes.
6. Witches.

NOTE YOUR NUMBER OF POINTS HERE

#8

You see that skeleton on the grid? He's so dumb that he'll fire his bow at you even if a creature stands between you two. Can you find the best place to stand so that, while trying to hit you, he kills as many monsters as possible?

(Skeletons fire in straight and diagonal lines. They can shoot down several monsters with a single arrow, but their projectiles don't ricochet off walls.)

Everything has the potential to be used as a weapon, as long as you're clever. Rank these weapons from the one inflicting the most damage to the one inflicting the least.

1. A wooden sword.
2. A wooden axe.
3. A wooden shovel.
4. A wooden pickaxe.

A weapon's damage is one thing, but don't forget its hitting speed!

#10

My skin is gray as a rock.

Most often I wield an axe.

In a building I stand.

I look like a villager.

Who am I?

NOTE YOUR NUMBER OF POINTS HERE

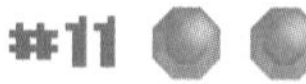

Answering questions is nice and all, but let's not forget your equipment.

With this inventory, what can you craft?

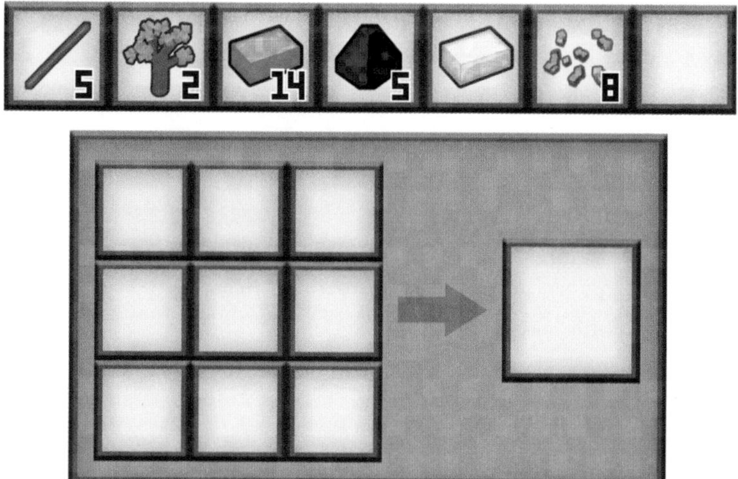

1. One sword, one iron helmet, and one iron chestplate.
2. One sword, one iron chestplate, and one pair of iron boots.
3. One iron chestplate, one iron helmet, and iron leggings.

#12

During your travels, you will certainly run into baby zombies. Don't let them get to you—they are nasty little monsters. Do you know their defining characteristic?

1. They cannot wear armor.
2. They can steal items.
3. They do not burn in the sun.

#13

What is a witch always holding in her hands?

1. Redstone powder.
2. Nothing. Her arms are crossed.
3. A vial of potion.

#14

In addition to being relatively stupid, skeletons are easily frightened. Do you know what they fear the most?

1. Dogs.
2. Chickens.
3. Ocelots.

"Herobrine" was also a valid answer, but I didn't want to make it too easy for you!

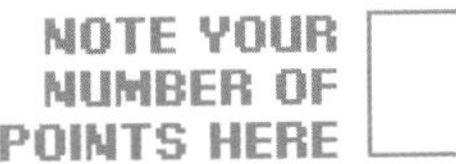

#15 

Oh, what a shame. . . . A bunch of villagers have been turned into zombies! Find them all before you start swinging. Who knows, maybe you could cure them later. . . .

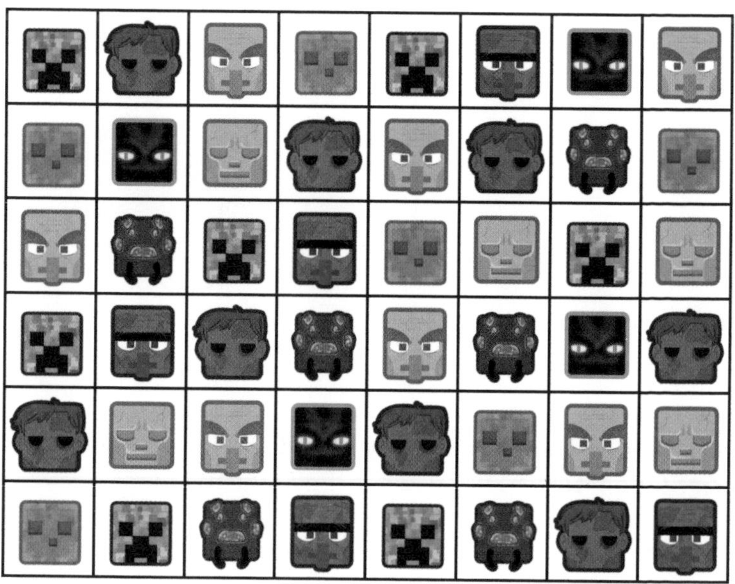

NOTE YOUR NUMBER OF POINTS HERE

Here we are! You have just concluded the first part of your quest. To reach the first Endercube puzzle, you need to be at least level 5, which means having accumulated no fewer than 100 experience points.

Your number of points is: ______

In order to proceed to the Endercube, you need a minimum of:

100 points.

If you don't yet meet the requirement, I suggest you try to answer the difficult questions again and make sure you remember everything!

I hope you won't disappoint me. . . .

ENDERCUBE PUZZLE #1

At last, behold the Endercube! As I explained before we started the trials, it is protected by three extremely powerful magical shells. You will have to combine your meager intellect with the experience you've gained thus far in order to solve the puzzle of this protective barrier. By the way, your predecessor—who also wanted to inherit my legacy—tried to force the Endercube open. You see that fine layer of dust? It's all that's left of him. I'm counting on you to rack your brain instead of acting impulsively!

I assume that, despite your general ignorance, you're familiar with sudoku? This first puzzle works the same way. By holding the Endercube in your hands, you will be able to feel its power vibrate and resound within you. If you are not strong enough, this power will annihilate you.

ENDERCUBE PUZZLE #1

Each picture can only be present once per line, once per column, and once per region.

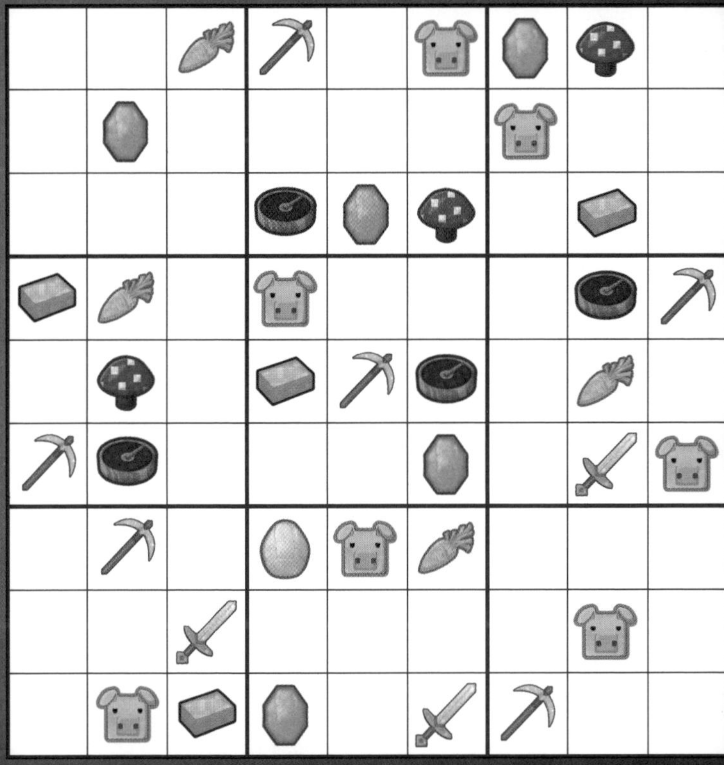

Have you managed to solve the puzzle? If so, turn the page. . . .

You made it!
The first shell unlocks!

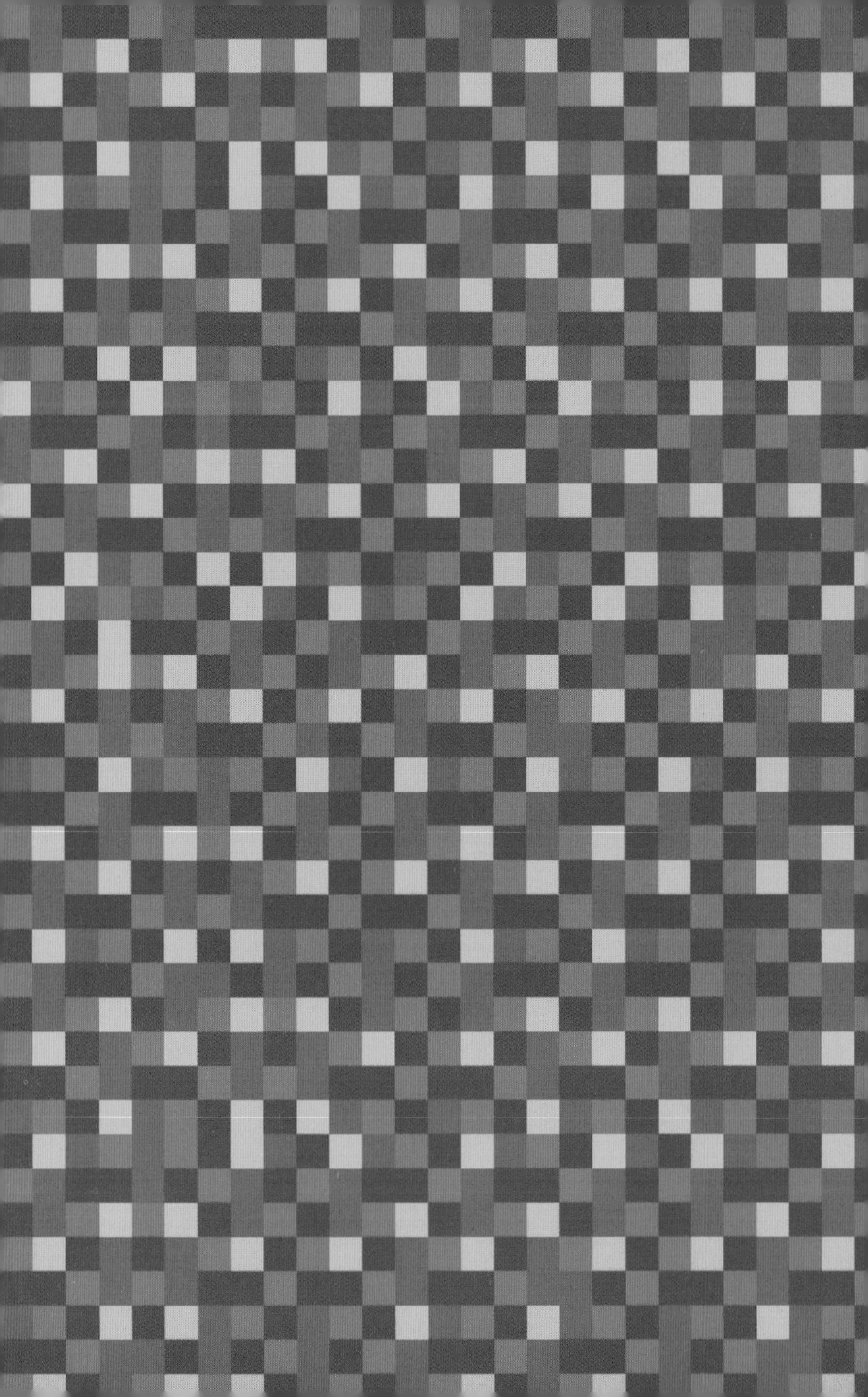

INITIATE

THE EXPLORATION TRIAL

As I said in the previous exploration trial, you will now enter the Nether. There are many things to know about this parallel world, on many different subjects.

The Nether is a hostile place where every moving thing will try to tear you apart. I've spent many long days in the suffocating heat, both to strengthen myself and to enlist the most horrible monsters for my battles.

But don't sweat it! If you succumb to the heat or your enemies, I'll just reanimate you as a zombie so you can become my eternal servant.

#1

Earlier, I asked you to craft a map. In order to better view your surroundings, you'll need to be able to zoom out to a full map. What is missing from the crafting table below to do so?

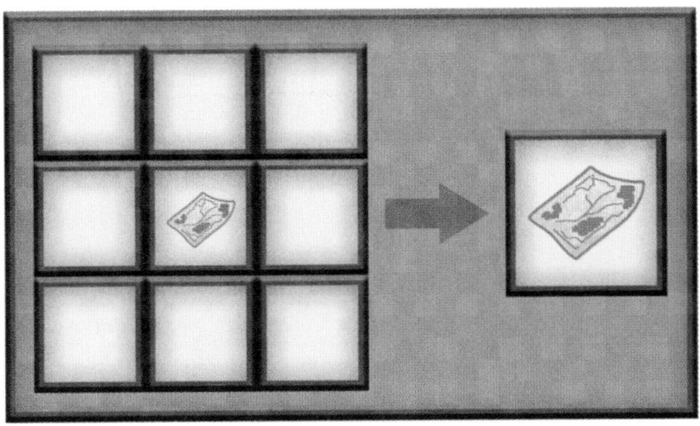

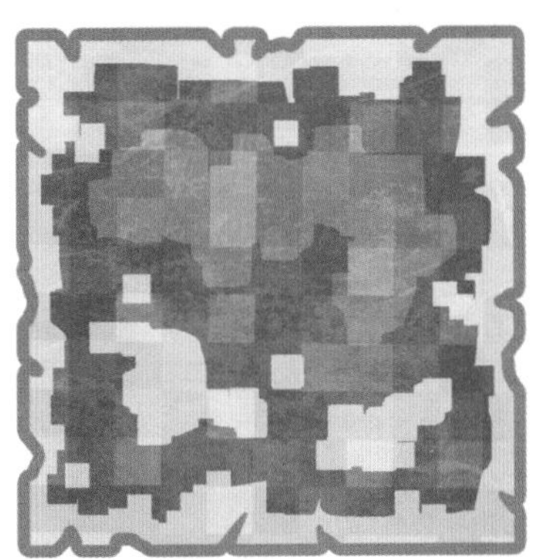

NOTE YOUR NUMBER OF POINTS HERE

#2

Once the teleportation dizziness fades, you come face to face with a zombie pigman. If you attack him, what will happen?

1. He will follow you everywhere, even if you leave through the Nether portal.
2. The zombie pigman will gain a lot of strength.
3. All zombie pigmen in the area will attack you.

Even if they look dumb, zombie pigmen are extremely dangerous.

#3

The Nether is a nice and welcoming place—well OK, for people like you, it may seem hellish and exhausting. Incidentally, it's impossible to sleep in the Nether, since any kind of bed automatically explodes. Do you know why?

1. Beds burst into flames because of the burning atmosphere of the Nether.
2. Beds burst into flames and explode in order to avoid a temporal shift with the Overworld.
3. Beds burst into flames and explode because they're cursed by ghasts.

When I venture into the Nether, I never forget to bring this specific object. Can you guess what it is?

1. Flint and steel.
2. A bucket of water.
3. A piston.
4. A compass.

Thanks to my superior intelligence, I know every element present in Minecraft. Since you can't relate, you'll just have to practice. Among these blocks, several cannot be found in the Nether. Which ones?

1. Lava blocks.
2. Magma blocks.
3. Quartz blocks.
4. Glowstone blocks.
5. Flame blocks.
6. Coarse dirt blocks.
7. Granite blocks.
8. Netherrack blocks.

NOTE YOUR NUMBER OF POINTS HERE

Once in the Nether, the Source Code has a radically different architecture. That explains the visual differences between this realm and the Overworld—and also why it's so dangerous. Even people like you who can't sense the Source itself should feel these fluctuations.

#6 

There are fortresses in the Nether. They are not as complex and vicious as the ones I create, but at least they have different kinds of rooms. Among the chambers below, which one does not belong in a Nether fortress?

1. A blaze spawner room.
2. A lava pit room.
3. A ghast spawner room.

#7  

Distances in the Nether are different than the Overworld. When you move forward one block in the Nether, how many blocks in the Overworld do you travel?

1. Six.
2. Eight.
3. Ten.

With the setup below, what might happen?

1. Nothing at all: neither the occupant nor the minecart will cross the Nether portal.
2. The minecart will cross the Nether portal but the occupant won't.
3. The occupant will cross the Nether portal but the minecart won't.

Lazy I can understand. But this is over the top, don't you think?

I enjoy strolling through fortresses—you can find some interesting chests, like this one. Only some joker added loot that doesn't belong in this kind of chest. Which items?

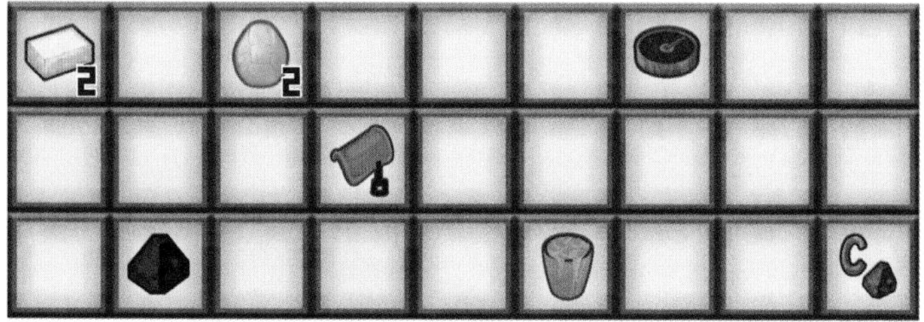

Nether portals are very strange. Do you even know what happens in the Overworld once you cross their disturbing violet veils?

1. Some events happen faster in the Overworld (weather, explosions, etc.).
2. Some events are paused in the Overworld (weather, explosions, etc.).
3. Some events are just canceled (weather, explosions, etc.).

Personally, I love to explore and find new things to obliterate or enslave. There's nothing sweeter! But since you are not me, you'll need to take some precautions. If you're not careful, some monsters might cross the Nether portal and get in the Overworld. Which of the following monsters are capable of such travel?

1. Ghasts.
2. Zombie pigmen.
3. Blazes.
4. Wither skeletons.

NOTE YOUR NUMBER OF POINTS HERE

You see that block? It's called soul sand. You can find it in the Nether, and it has very peculiar properties. Which of the following statements is accurate?

1. It slows you down as well as all other creatures.
2. It slows you down and makes you lose health with every step.
3. You slowly sink into it, and your equipment loses some durability.

There are lots of faces on this block. Holy mushroom cow! Isn't that Robert? He's one of your predecessors who tried to obtain my powers.

#13 

In the Overworld, I'm found.

In the Nether, I'm not.

When I'm placed therein, I disappear.

Endermen fear me.

What am I?

#14 

One of the objects below will help you find north in the Nether. Which one?

1. A compass.
2. The position of the portal.
3. A block of netherrack.

NOTE YOUR NUMBER OF POINTS HERE

#15

You're on the verge of demise, and you need to find the portal to get out of the Nether as soon as possible. Unfortunately, a ghast has destroyed the crossings. You must place Nether bricks to make your way back, but you have only four of them. Be careful of the zombie pigmen: if you walk within a block of them, they'll attack.

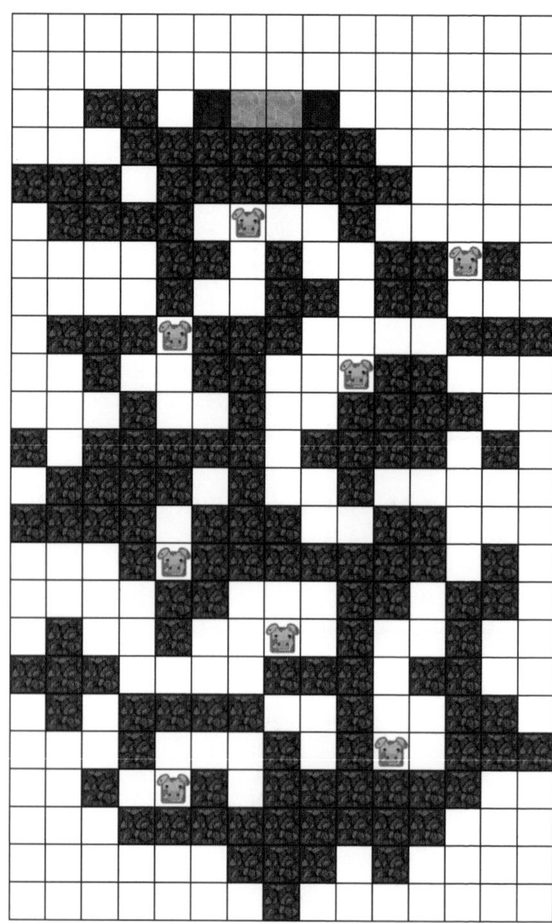

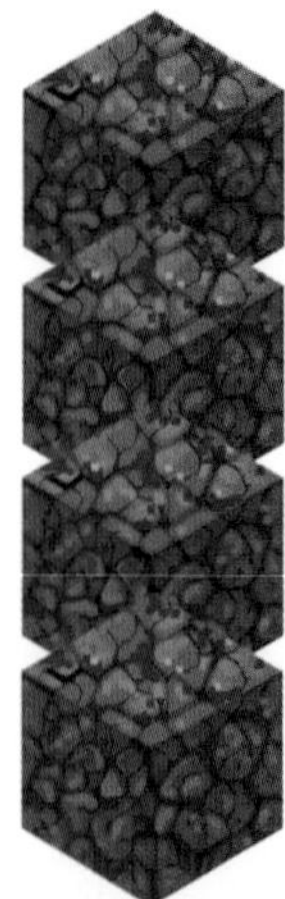

NOTE YOUR NUMBER OF POINTS HERE

Exploring the Nether is a good way to strengthen your spirits and see if you have what it takes. You look promising, but I fear you still have some serious weaknesses. We're far from over: with the next trials, I'll be able to better determine your capabilities.

Let's see if you can advance to level 6.

Your number of points is: 

In order to proceed to the building trial, you need at least:

15 points.

THE BUILDING TRIAL

Since it appears you can find your way around the Nether without stumbling into lava or being torn to shreds, let's see if you can construct some buildings and consolidate your defenses. Of course, you'll never gain expertise like Master Crafters or even yours truly, but I expect you to put your heart into it! Prepare your building schematics and put that pint-size cranium of yours to work!!

#1 

First things first: what do you absolutely need to build near the Nether portal leading to the Overworld?

1. A separation chamber.
2. A beacon.
3. An XP tower.

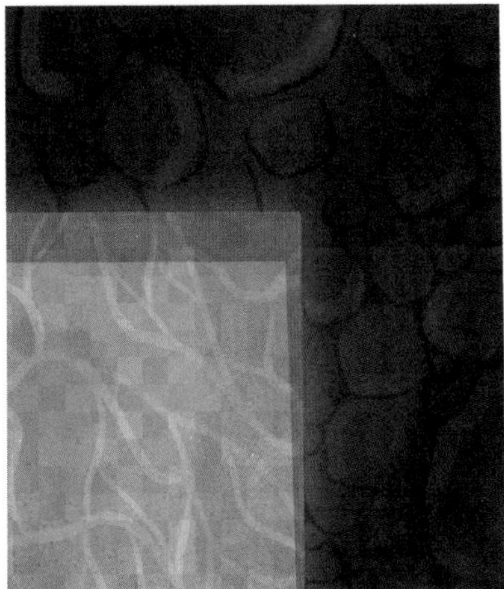

#2 

There are a gazillion possible items to craft in Minecraft. In the list below, which item does not exist?

1. The anvil.
2. The wall.
3. The shelf.
4. The carpet.

NOTE YOUR NUMBER OF POINTS HERE

When you start wandering in parallel worlds, potions become essential. But you need a brewing stand to make them! What is missing from the crafting table to build one?

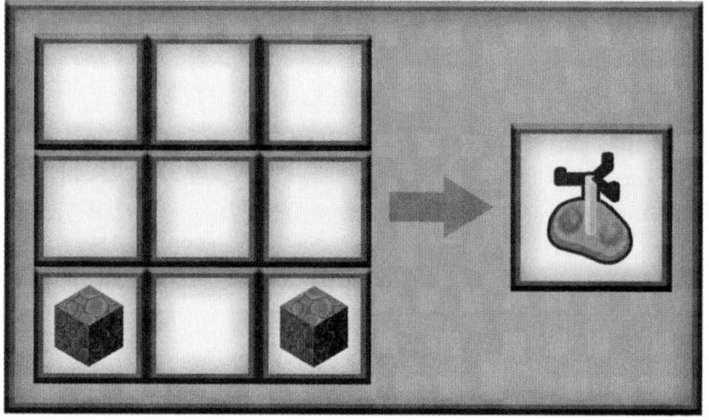

This is one of my favorite tools. If you only knew the horrors I can create with my foul mixtures, you wouldn't be able to sleep at night!

In the list below, you'll find some objects that are not power components (meaning they don't produce redstone power). Can you identify which ones?

1. A lever.
2. A daylight sensor.
3. A repeater.
4. A pressure plate.
5. A piston.
6. A redstone wire.

Shoot! There are several things missing from this inventory that are required to build a bookshelf—which will be vital to enchant your tools and weapons. What are you lacking?

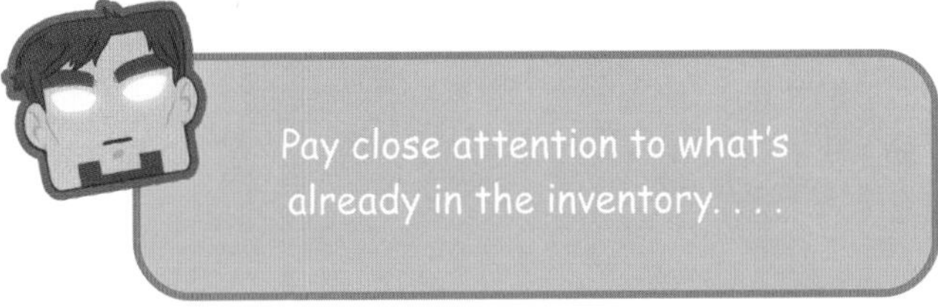

NOTE YOUR NUMBER OF POINTS HERE

In the Nether, Snowkin the snow golem would be useless, since he'd keep suffering damage until he disappeared. But this isn't an issue for iron golems, whose strength is truly impressive. What do you know about this creature?

1. It moves slowly, can't open doors, and normally spawns in villages.
2. It moves slowly, can climb ladders, and attacks ghasts.
3. It can't open doors, can climb ladders, and always holds a red flower in its hand.

At first glance, all of the houses below look alike. But don't be fooled: they're slightly different and each house has one identical match. It's up to you to pair them!

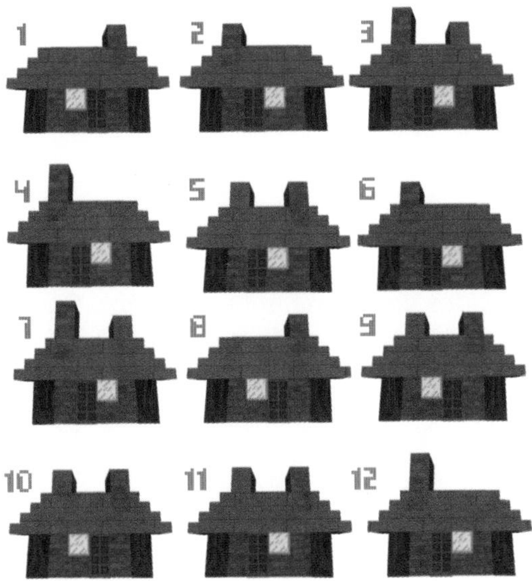

Those are the kind of dull buildings my minions would destroy in a matter of seconds. You've no doubt heard of these fierce monsters who've fought many battles on my behalf. All villagers tremble at the mere thought that I could unleash these horrors on their settlements.

NOTE YOUR NUMBER OF POINTS HERE

#8

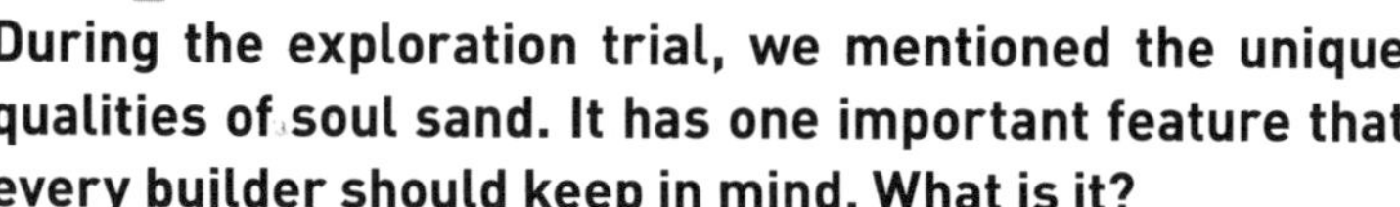

During the exploration trial, we mentioned the unique qualities of soul sand. It has one important feature that every builder should keep in mind. What is it?

1. A block is only seven-eighths of the normal block height.
2. You cannot put anything on these blocks.
3. These blocks cannot be placed in the Overworld.

#9

Building bookshelves is one thing; placing them intelligently is another. Since your goal is to maximize the strength of an enchanting table, how many bookshelves do you need to place to make use of its full power?

1. Eight.
2. Twelve.
3. Fifteen.

We will soon see if you're familiar with enchanting!

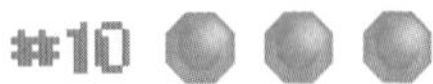

At first glance, redstone seems very complex, but it is essential to master it. In the image below, you are about to place a block. Which one will turn off the redstone power?

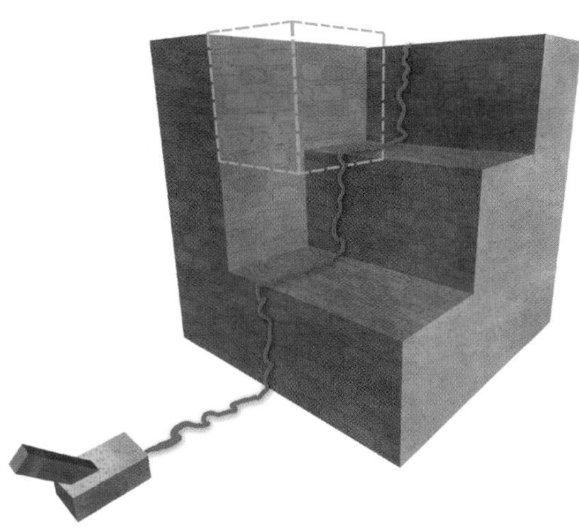

1. A glass block.
2. A cobblestone block.
3. A piston.

Endlessly, I illuminate.

Snow, I melt.

Gently, I must be handled.

What am I?

Traps are very useful for protecting your buildings. The dispenser block is one of the best for setting up defenses. Everybody knows it can fire arrows at your enemies, but you can be more inventive than that! What will happen if I place a TNT block in a dispenser?

1. The TNT block will be launched three to five blocks away, primed for explosion.
2. The TNT block will be launched three to five blocks away, without activation.
3. The TNT block will be placed in front of the dispenser, primed for explosion.
4. The TNT block will be placed in front of the dispenser, without activation.

I think you're ready to start decorating your house. Considering your bad taste, I'm sure you'll want to put paintings everywhere. All in all, there are twenty-six possible designs. In the list that follows, one doesn't exist in Minecraft. Which one?

1. The Pool.
2. Bonjour, Monsieur Courbet.
3. Kebab.
4. Hamburger.
5. Fighters.

The only paintings I enjoy looking at are the ones depicting me!

NOTE YOUR NUMBER OF POINTS HERE

#14

Not all elements react the same when they come in contact with a piston block. For each object below, tell me if it is pushed, destroyed, transformed, or unaffected.

1. An anvil.
2. Some packed ice.
3. A bed.
4. A furnace.
5. A jack o'lantern.
6. A melon.

#15

By exploring, harvesting, and killing new creatures, you will gather more and more loot that you'll need to store and organize. Item frames are useful visual indicators when you put them above a chest. One of the following statements about item frames is wrong. Which one?

1. Watches and compasses work normally inside an item frame.
2. Item frames are not blocks but entities.
3. The object displayed in the frame can be rotated six times.
4. When a map is placed inside, an item frame occupies the full side of the block it is placed on.

NOTE YOUR NUMBER OF POINTS HERE

The Nether brings new possibilities in terms of building. I'm glad I managed to get that information into your feeble brain! Apparently, you have enough talent and know-how to construct an acceptable base. Interesting. And you haven't given up yet. This reminds me of someone. . . .

You are almost halfway to the end of your quest, but you have your work cut out for you. You can reach level 7 if you have a minimum of 35 experience points.

Your number of points is: 

In order to progress to the farming trial, you need a minimum of:

35 points.

If that's not the case, keep practicing before you continue!

THE FARMING TRIAL

During the previous farming trial, you showed some aptitude for agriculture. Unfortunately it is far, far, far from being enough for me. There are so many things to know in this domain, and we've barely scratched the surface. I want you to be able to automate your crops and grow any plant in any place in the Overworld . . . and even the Nether! You'll need more than just a few seeds and a bucket of water for that!

#1 

You can't pour water in the Nether: it evaporates instantly due to the heat. But there is a way to store it. How?

1. With a bucket.
2. With a cauldron.
3. With a vial.

#2

In the Nether, there are some very special plants: Nether warts. You can grow them in other realms, notably the Overworld, but they require one specific condition. What is it?

1. The warts must be placed on a block of soul sand.
2. The warts must grow in the dark.
3. The warts must be far away from any water source.

Don't forget: if you disappoint me, I can easily curse you by having these warts grow all over your body!

NOTE YOUR NUMBER OF POINTS HERE

#3 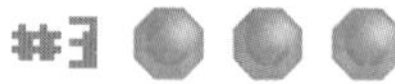

All the objects below are directly linked to farming and cattle breeding. Can you name them all?

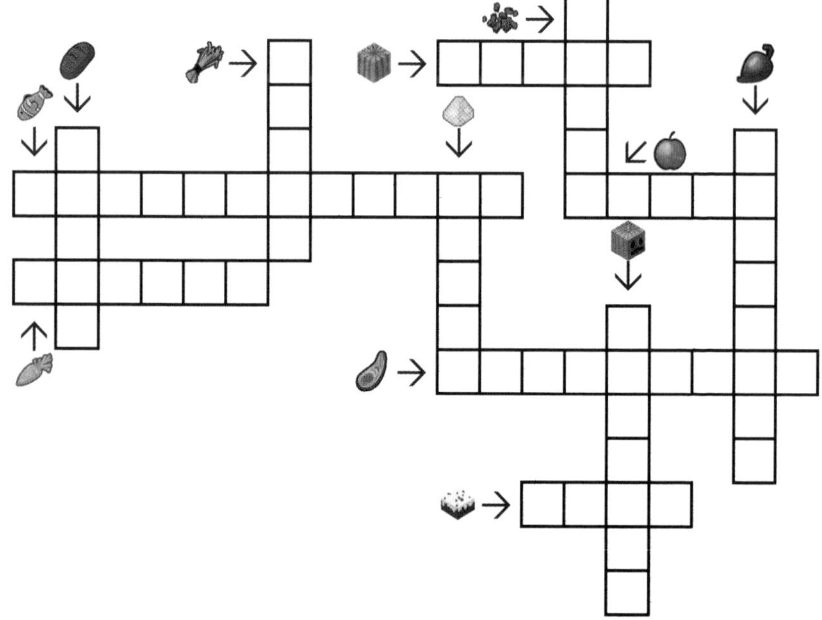

#4

Light is as important as water for farming. Without it, many plants won't grow. One of the following statements is true: which one?

1. A jack o'lantern is so bright that it uproots mushrooms.
2. Trees can't grow in the dark, even if there is a torch nearby.
3. Glowstone can illuminate your crops so that they keep growing at night.

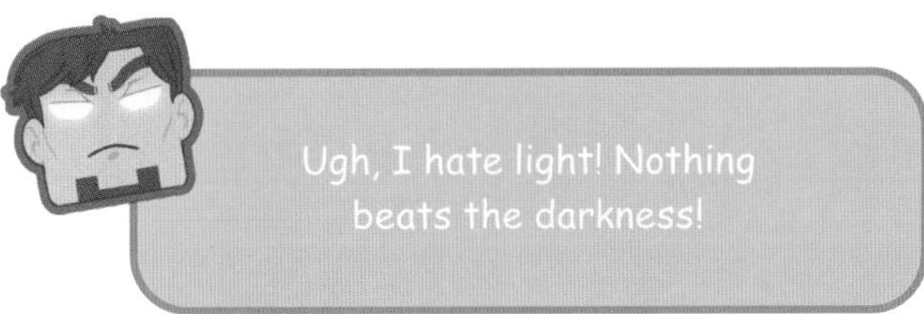

NOTE YOUR NUMBER OF POINTS HERE

Like I said, I still eat from time to time. In the crafting table below, you'll find my favorite recipe. What does it make?

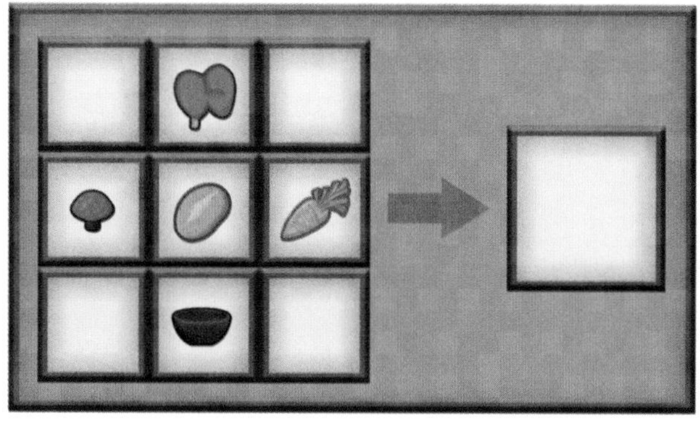

1. Carrot soup.
2. Rabbit stew.
3. Roast chicken.

#6  

You may not know this fact (but for your own sake, I hope you do): there is a so-called saturation level of every kind of food. Unlike your hunger, you cannot see your saturation level. How can you tell if it reaches zero?

1. You start losing health points.
2. When you eat, the restoration effect of food is doubled.
3. Your hunger level starts to drop.

#7  

It can be very useful to breed livestock and eat them, but you can also adopt a travel companion, like a wolf. Once tamed, it can have cubs with another wolf under which condition?

1. The wolves must be at full health.
2. The wolves must be fed only with rabbit meat.
3. The wolves must sit side by side.

NOTE YOUR NUMBER OF POINTS HERE

One thing is certain, I'm not meant to live with other beings. As far as I'm concerned, nothing beats a solitary life. I just can't stand the idea of having a pet around me, wasting my time. And I know what I'm talking about. I tried it once, and, believe me, it didn't last long!

When looking at the optimized wheat crops below, any noob could easily spot which essential element is missing. How about you?

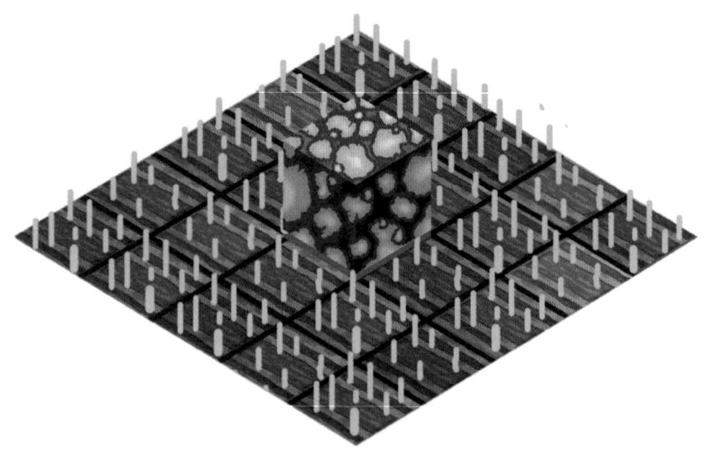

Mushroom cows are truly bizarre creatures. Of the following claims, which is true?

1. You can shave mushroom cows and milk them with a wooden bowl.
2. You can milk mushroom cows and breed them with normal cows.
3. You can shave mushroom cows and speed up the regrowth of their mushrooms with bone meal.

Honestly, some creatures are bordering on ridiculous. . . .

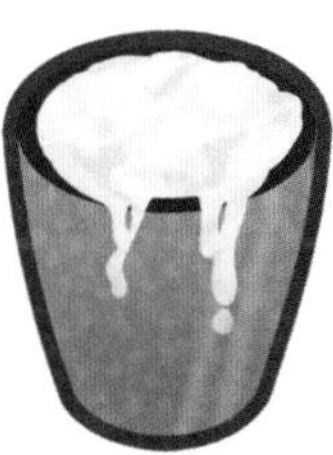

NOTE YOUR NUMBER OF POINTS HERE

#10

If you want to go fishing and don't have any water sources near your home, I suggest you create one. As with farming or cattle breeding, fishing is a good source of food. You can even find treasure in the water! What does the "Lure" enchantment do to a fishing rod?

1. It reduces the wait time between two catches.
2. It increases the chances of getting treasure.
3. It allows you to get two catches at once.

Among the following food items, which is the best to satisfy your hunger?

1. Cooked mutton.
2. A carrot.
3. An enchanted golden apple.
4. Cooked pork chop.

These food items aren't so bad. Honestly, you're lucky that cabbage and broccoli don't exist in Minecraft.

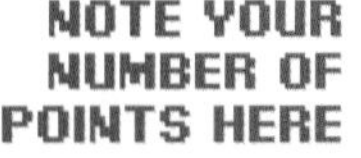

If you plan to travel long distances, you'll need to tame a horse and understand its behaviors. You can feed a horse with several kinds of food. For each item in the list, find its corresponding attribute.

1. Golden carrot.
2. Hay bale.
3. Golden apple.
4. Sugar.
5. Melon.

A. Activates love mode in tamed horses.
B. No particular effect.
C. Activates love mode in tamed horses.
D. Cannot be given to a horse.
E. Cannot be given to an untamed horse.

You need to be able to spot the smallest details in the blink of an eye. There are seven differences between these two images. Can you find them?

NOTE YOUR NUMBER OF POINTS HERE

#14 

Sometimes even your enemies deserve special treatment . . . like offering them poisoned food. I've disposed of countless kings this way. One of the following food items has a 30% chance of poisoning whoever ingests it. Which is it?

1. A pufferfish.
2. A spider eye.
3. Raw chicken.
4. A poisonous potato.

#15

What might happen if you put some bone meal on a grass block?

1. Nothing—it's useless.
2. Flowers will grow in a seven-block radius.
3. Any plant, including trees, will grow in a seven-block radius.

NOTE YOUR NUMBER OF POINTS HERE

Nothing too hard in this trial. So you can grow a few plants? Big deal. You need to really impress me, and, for now, you haven't. At least I won't have to hand-feed you from now until you finish these challenges (though you'd starve before I stooped to that level).

It's time to take a look at your progress. If you exceed my expectations—which are incredibly low—your destiny might just be more glorious than a melon farmer! If your total experience is at least 55 points, you'll be able to move on to level 8.

Your number of points is: 

In order to go on to the mining trial, you need:

55 points.

THE MINING TRIAL

The Nether is an incredibly dangerous and infernal underground domain. Getting there is certainly traumatizing, but it can also teach a few lessons. What's more, your sensory capacities increase considerably in this vast, dark, and lethal environment. I'm sure this will sharpen your miner's instinct even further. We'll find out soon enough.

#1 

Pay attention! We'll start with a role-playing exercise: You've barely started mining in the Nether when lava flow falls right on your head. You've got bad luck, sure, but you're also on fire. You use your cauldron of water to extinguish the fire and save your last hit points. What amount of water will you have left?

1. None, the cauldron is empty.
2. Half the cauldron.
3. Two-thirds of the cauldron.

Extinguishing the flames?
You've got the wits of a slime!
Fire is good for you!

NOTE YOUR NUMBER OF POINTS HERE

At this point, you need to start enchanting your tools. There are some very useful enchantments for your pickaxe, like "Fortune." Besides the experience points you've gathered, something else is needed when using an enchanting table. What is it?

Desperate times call for desperate measures in the Nether. And you'll be in trouble more often than not. I bet if you broke your pickaxe, you'd even try to mine soul sand with your sword. If you did, how fast would it wear out?

1. Three times faster than normal.
2. One and a half times faster than normal.
3. Two times faster than normal.

The enchantment "Silk Touch" enables you to gather blocks that are usually destroyed when you try to mine them. For which of the blocks below is that the case?

1. Ice.
2. Glowstone.
3. Sugar cane.
4. Iron ore.
5. Monsters spawner.

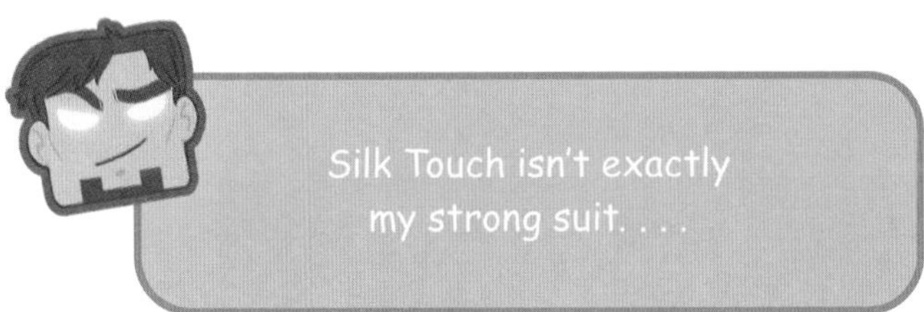

NOTE YOUR NUMBER OF POINTS HERE

A trip to the Nether is a great way to discover new blocks. Nevertheless, you'll need to know how much time it takes to mine each of them in order to save precious time in such a hostile environment. Which of these blocks is easiest to mine with your bare hands?

1. The netherrack.
2. The soul sand.
3. The Nether quartz.
4. The glowstone.

Have you ever seen more splendid shades of blocks? In my case, yes: in the End. The colors are just incredible. But we'll get to that later. . . .

#6

A group of zombie pigmen is starting to pay a little too much attention to you. . . . You'll need to hurry and pick up the pieces of quartz and glowstone that you see illustrated below. Note that in order to pick them up, you must draw four straight lines passing through the block on which they are located.

(You cannot lift your pencil once during the drawing. Diagonal lines are allowed.)

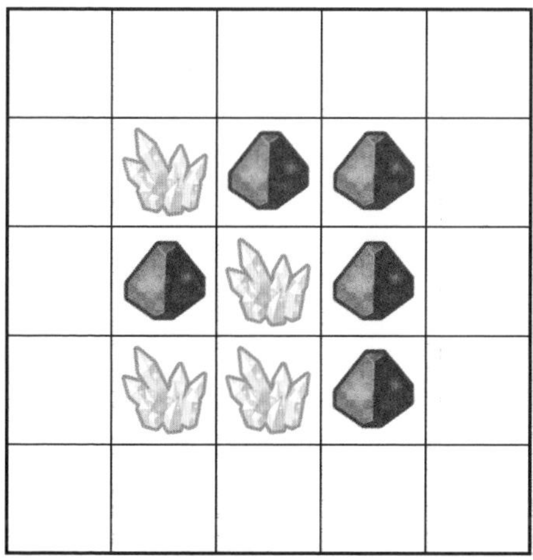

Now that's what I call a riddle!

NOTE YOUR NUMBER OF POINTS HERE

#7 

In the list below, which enchantments would be useless for your shovel or your pickaxe?

1. "Fortune."
2. "Sharpness."
3. "Unbreaking."
4. "Looting."
5. "Mending."

The Endercube is protected by many enchantments that only I can undo. Some of them were created by directly accessing the Source Code—needless to say, you'll never be able to reproduce them. My legacy is far too precious to fall into the hands of some fool!

It's not uncommon for people to venture to the Nether solely to gather quartz. Which of the following statements do you think best defines this ore?

1. The quartz is pretty common, like iron ore.
2. The quartz is pretty rare, like gold ore.
3. The quartz is very rare, like diamond ore.

We haven't yet talked about shovels, but they're absolutely essential tools. You can even find them in the game; do you know how?

(Several answers are possible.)

1. By killing a zombie.
2. By looting a fortress.
3. By searching a chest in an abandoned mineshaft.
4. By trading with villagers.

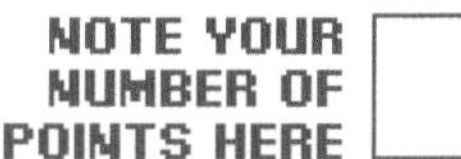

#10  

I'd like you to build a TNT minecart, just in case. To do so, complete the two crafting tables below in order.

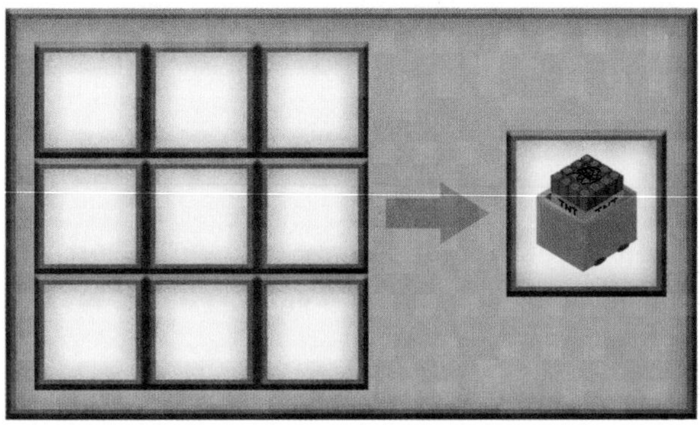

If you're wondering why you'd ever need such a minecart, I have a very simple answer for you: "BOOOOOOOOOM!!!"

#11

Netherrack has been the subject of much speculation. If you want to become a good miner, you need to know every little fact about every block in Minecraft. According to you, why is this rock red?

1. It's soaked with blood.
2. It's covered with moss.
3. It's hot and withered.

#12

You've just prepared these three furnaces. But the fire may go out in one of them before it has finished smelting. Which one am I talking about?

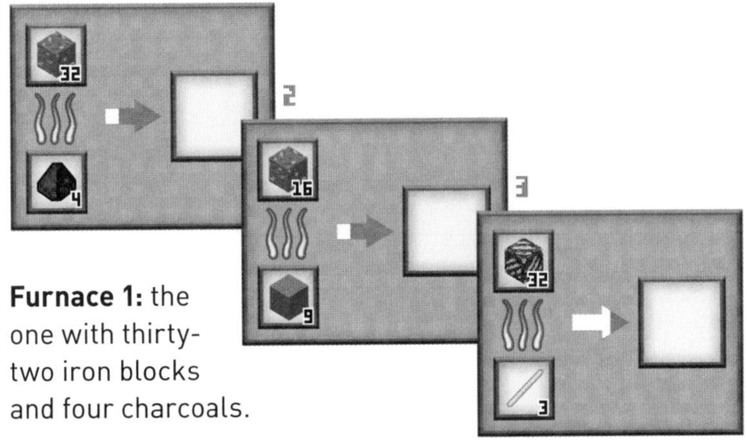

Furnace 1: the one with thirty-two iron blocks and four charcoals.

Furnace 2: the one with sixteen gold blocks and nine planks.

Furnace 3: the one with thirty-two quartz ore and three blaze rods.

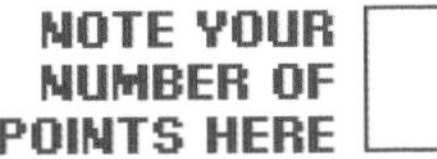

If you want to bulk up your forearms, it might be a good idea to mine obsidian with your bare hands. How long will it take?

1. Two minutes and twenty seconds.
2. Four minutes and ten seconds.
3. Seven minutes and thirty-five seconds.

With a diamond axe, it takes only ten seconds. . . .

Here's an idea for linking your Nether portal to a spot filled with resources: use rails. What's missing from the inventory below to build one minecart, forty-eight rails, and one powered rail?

NOTE YOUR NUMBER OF POINTS HERE

Speaking of rails, if you want to use them in the Nether, you'll need to build something special. What is it?

1. Powered rails so that you don't stop in your tracks.
2. A redstone circuit to control traffic on your railway.
3. A tunnel covering the whole railway.

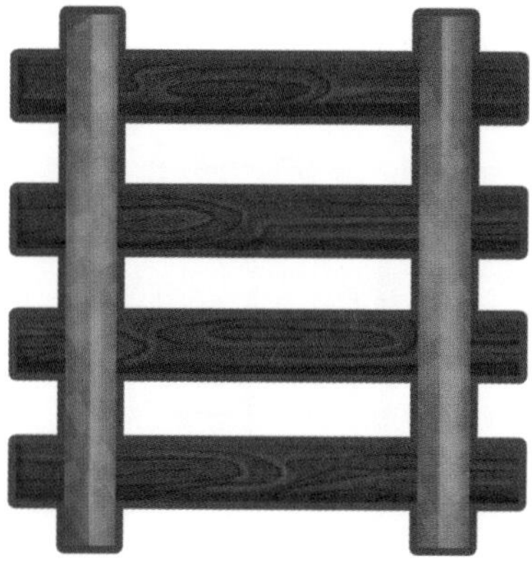

NOTE YOUR NUMBER OF POINTS HERE

You will soon face the terrible Endercube again. What? You don't really feel like it? What a shame! I guess I'd be terrified too, if I had your skill level!

In any case, keep tracking your progress—and don't cheat! I've put an enchantment on the cube to detect your lies. Believe me, you don't want to know what happens if you do!

You will need 80 experience points to pass on to level 9.

Your number of points is: 

In order to proceed to the combat trial, you must have a minimum of:

80 points.

THE COMBAT TRIAL

You hear that sound? Well, me neither! That means you haven't put on your armor, drawn your weapon, and run screaming at the monsters of the Nether!

So get on with it and prepare for combat as fast as you can! Do you think I became a great warrior by dawdling? Let's go!

#1

Here's one to get in the swing of things (pun intended). From the list of monsters below, tell me which ones you'd never come across in the Nether.

1. A blaze.
2. A creeper.
3. An enderman.
4. A wither.
5. A slime.

#2

Which of these weapons is useless in the Nether?

1. A bow with a "Flame" enchantment.
2. An axe with a "Sharpness" enchantment.
3. A sword with a "Smite" enchantment.

NOTE YOUR NUMBER OF POINTS HERE

Here is the crafting recipe of a very useful potion in the Nether. Do you know what it's called?

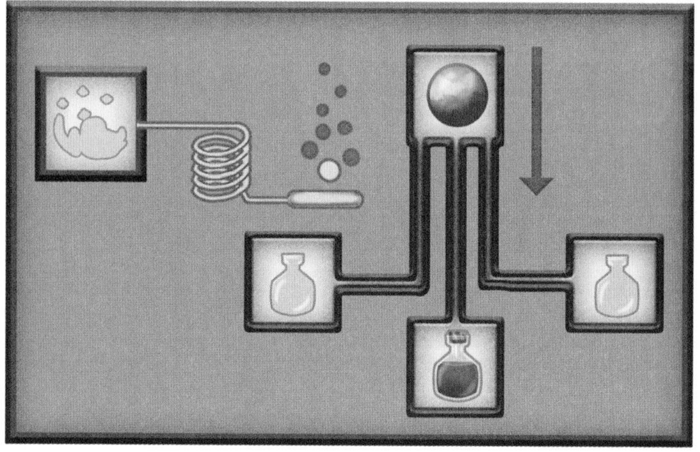

1. A potion of Instant Health.
2. A potion of Fire Resistance.
3. A potion of Strength.

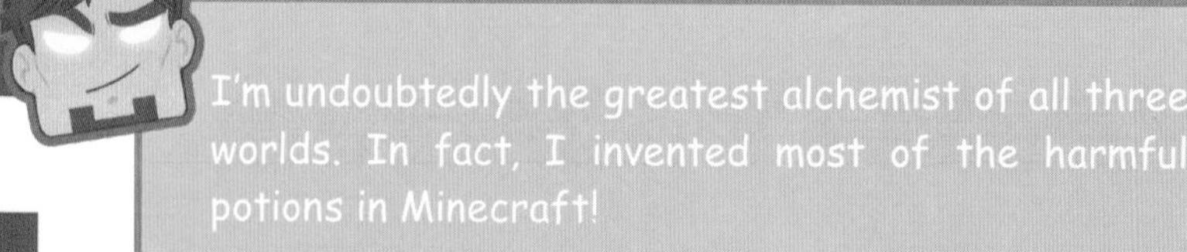

#4

Do you know the best trick for fighting ghasts?

1. Throw a splash potion at them.
2. Grab them with a fishing rod.
3. Throw them back their fireballs.

#5

"Know your enemy" is one of my favorite sayings. That's why I want you to match each of the attacks below with the corresponding monster.

1. Exploding fireball.
2. Sword strike.
3. Flaming fireball.
4. Jumping attack.
5. Total annihilation.

A. Magma cube.
B. Wither skeleton.
C. Blaze.
D. Ghast.
E. Herobrine.

Encountering new monsters can be a terrifying experience. Take wither skeletons, for instance: they're much more dangerous than their cousins from the Overworld! What happens if one of them hits you and inflicts the "Wither" status effect?

1. Your movement will be reduced.
2. The strength of your attacks will be reduced.
3. You'll receive damage over time and die.

Glitchwitch was very helpful when I began studying the Source of the Nether. Thanks to her, I easily learned how to twist its code, bending it to my will and forging my legend. For many adventurers, this arid world is synonymous with destruction and desolation. For me, it's been an extraordinary source of imagination and creation.

#7

You have looted so many objects from your enemies that you need to sort out your inventory. Place the remaining items correctly.

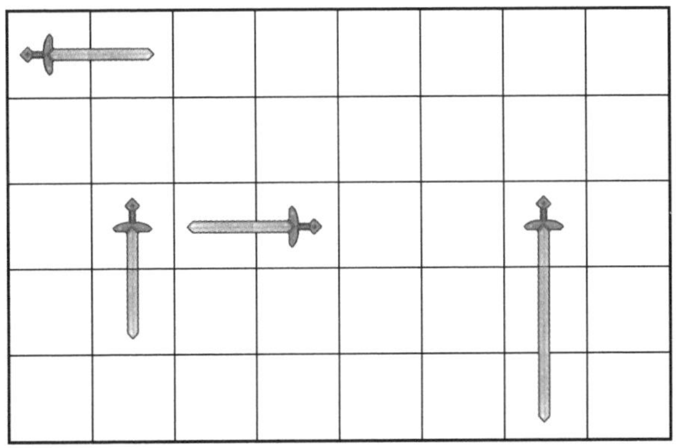

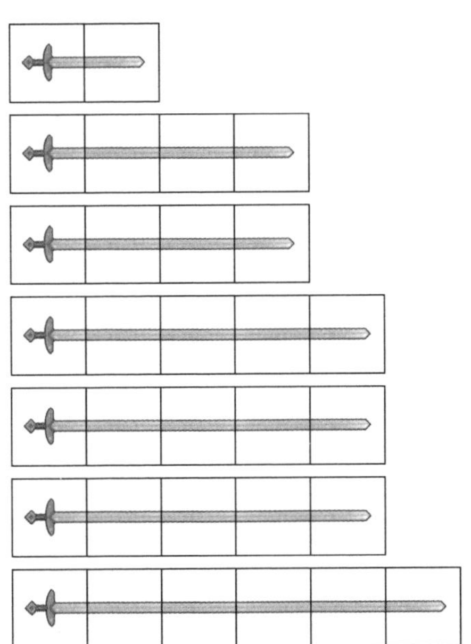

NOTE YOUR NUMBER OF POINTS HERE

The bow is an essential weapon in the Nether. Surely you know how to craft one by now, but what do you know about arrows? There are fourteen types in total. In the list below, find the ones that don't exist in Minecraft.

1. Spectral arrows.
2. Wither arrows.
3. Arrows of Strength.
4. Arrows of Healing.
5. Arrows of Paralysis.
6. Arrows of Night Vision.

Before trying to shoot at moving targets, you'd better train properly! Baby zombies are perfect for target practice: those speedy guys will put your reflexes to the test!

#9 

With their childish crying, ghasts are absolutely terrifying. What method can be used to temporarily immobilize these monsters so you can shoot them with a bow?

1. Make sure the ghast touches a glass block.
2. Make sure the ghast goes through a lava fall.
3. Launch a snowball at the ghast.
4. Throw the ghast's own fireballs back at it.

#10

How many levels of the "Sharpness" enchantment can you put on a weapon?

1. Three.
2. Four.
3. Five.

NOTE YOUR NUMBER OF POINTS HERE

It's time to proudly display your colors and customize your shield. The monsters will fear you much more! To do so, you must combine a customized banner with your shield. What is missing from the crafting table below to get the following pattern?

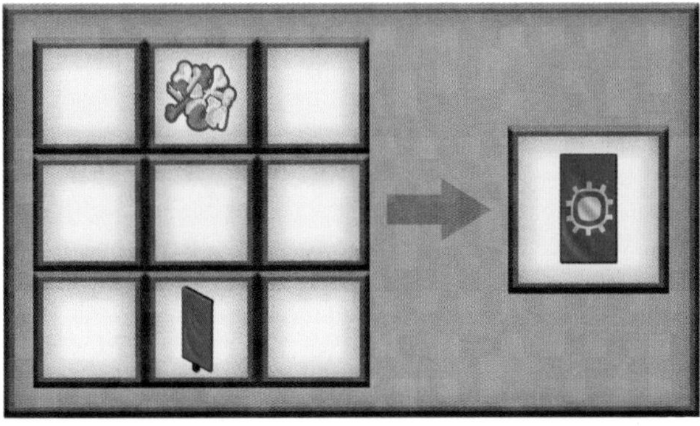

1. An oxeye daisy.
2. An azure bluet.
3. A sunflower.

#12

After several trips to the Nether, you might just be crazy enough to summon the terrible wither. What is missing from the summoning configuration below?

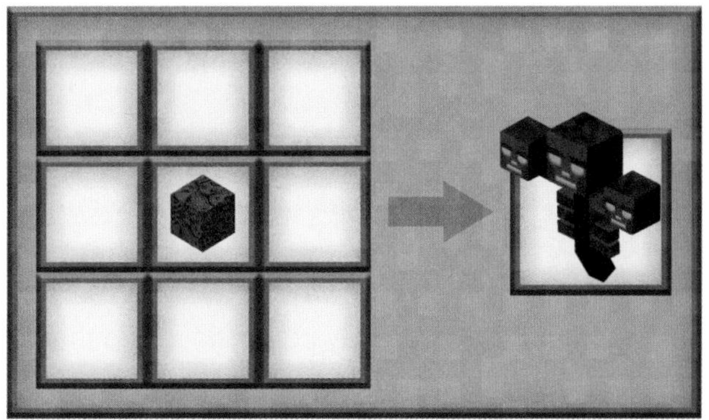

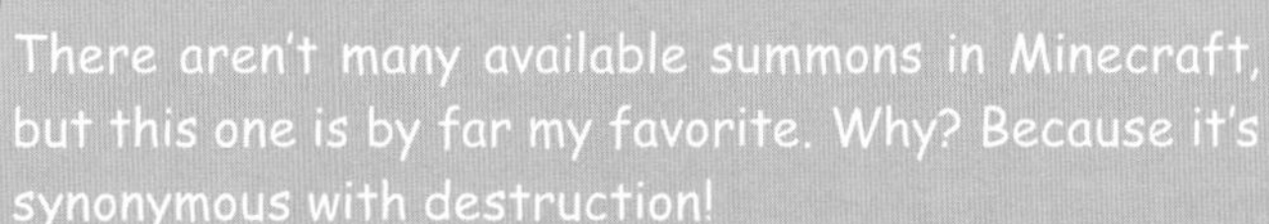

There aren't many available summons in Minecraft, but this one is by far my favorite. Why? Because it's synonymous with destruction!

NOTE YOUR NUMBER OF POINTS HERE

#13 

Withers are fearsome opponents. You need to know their strengths and weaknesses to better anticipate their moves during a fight. Which of the following statements is true?

1. Withers are immune to fire and lava, they will attack any creature except the undead, and their projectiles explode.
2. Withers are immune to melee combat, they will attack any creature, and their projectiles inflict the Wither status effect.
3. Withers regain some health when you throw a harming potion at them, they will only attack you, and their projectiles destroy any block they hit.

Now that's what I call devilish perfection!

#14

Fire and lava I do not fear.

To a fortress I stay near.

My heart is burning pure and clear.

What am I?

⎓╎リ↸╎リ⊣ ᒲ|| ⍑ᒷ╎∷

ᒲ╎⊣⍑ℸ ̣ ʖᒷ ᔑ

ꖎᒷリ⊣ℸ ̣⍑|| ᑑ⚍ᒷᓭℸ ̣

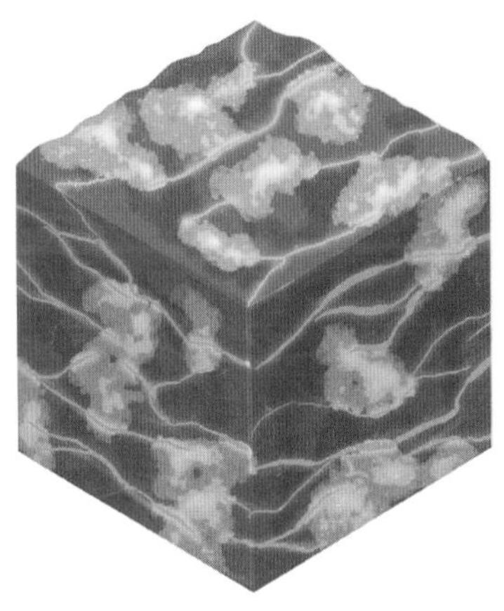

NOTE YOUR NUMBER OF POINTS HERE

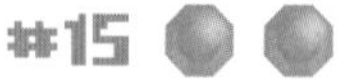

As you can see, a fight has gone south, and you're just about to take a nasty tumble deep into the Nether. Which item offers your best hope for survival?

1. An ender pearl.
2. Elytra.
3. A bucket of water.
4. Boots with the "Feather Falling" enchantment.

NOTE YOUR NUMBER OF POINTS HERE

You're still alive? I did not see that coming! You've clearly exceeded my expectations, succeeding where no one else before you could.

Now you must solve the second Endercube puzzle. From there you will to go the End—only there will you be able to complete your quest and access the core of the cube.

But first, let's see if you have enough experience to move on to level 10.

How many points do you have?

Your number of points is: 

To continue to the Endercube puzzle, you must have:

100 points.

ENDERCUBE PUZZLE #2

Here you are, at the Endercube's second puzzle. Say, is that . . . pride I'm feeling? No, no—probably just indigestion.

To unlock this barrier and continue to the final level, you'll need to find the correct path and reach the eye of ender. I hope your skills and knowledge have developed enough; otherwise, the final trials may take many attempts. If that's the case, you can always go back to train and better prepare yourself.

ENDERCUBE PUZZLE #2

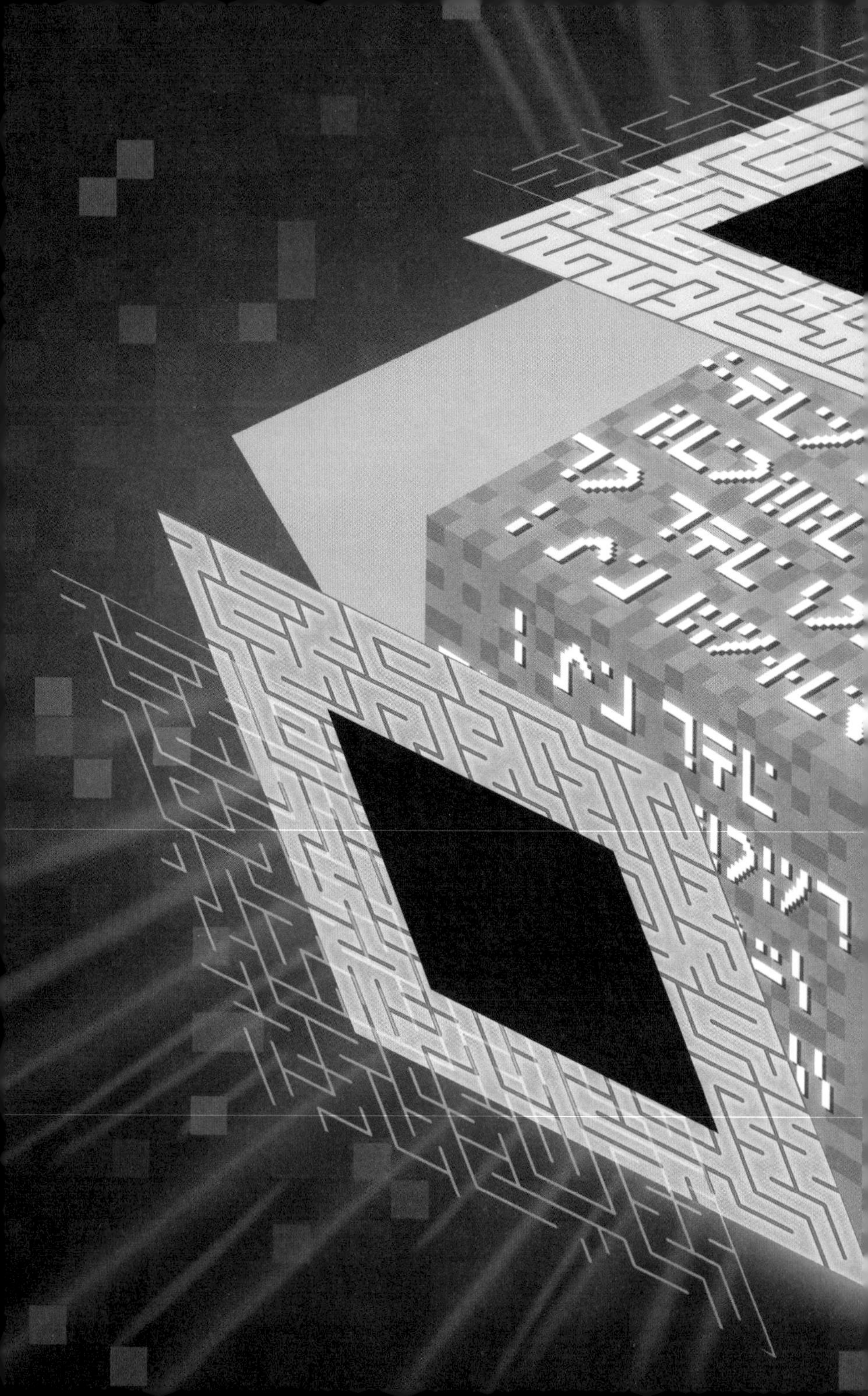

Did you get lost? Shocker. You'll need to use all three of your neurons to find the solution!
Did you find the right way? Then you may proceed. . .

EXPERT

THE EXPLORATION TRIAL

The End and I, we go way back. I'll tell you all about it as the trials go by. It's impressive that you made it here in one piece, but I don't want to get my hopes too high. If I did and you failed, I'd be even more disappointed. You're getting close to the goal, but that means you must be all the more careful. Exploring the End is incredibly dangerous. The Nether is a tropical island in comparison.

If you want to go to the End, you must know how to craft an eye of ender, which is needed to activate the portal. What is missing from the crafting table below?

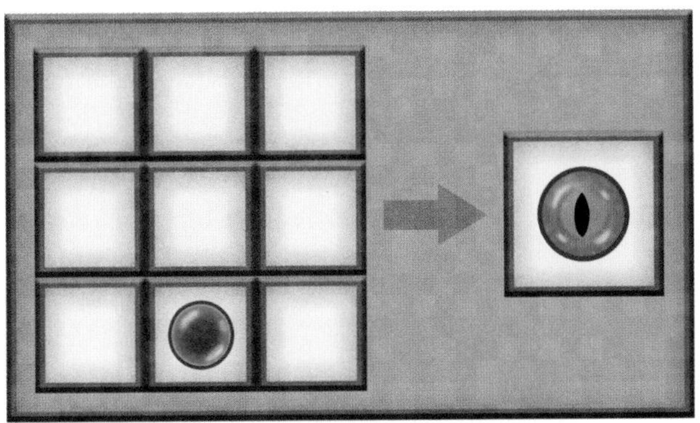

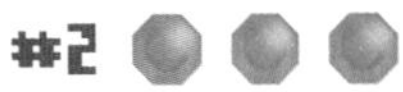

To craft an eye of ender, you'll have to first fight a certain number of endermen—a risky undertaking. To avoid unnecessary battles, you'd better know from the start how many eyes you'll need.

1. You need six eyes of ender to activate the portal.
2. You need nine eyes of ender to activate the portal.
3. You need twelve eyes of ender to activate the portal.

NOTE YOUR NUMBER OF POINTS HERE

#3 

So you've got your eyes of ender. That's useful, but it's not enough. Finding an End portal can be even harder, given how well they're hidden. Do you know how to find one?

1. You have to throw an ender pearl on an enderman, then follow him.
2. You have to throw an eye of ender in the air, and it will point the way.
3. You have to consult a map provided by a village cartographer.

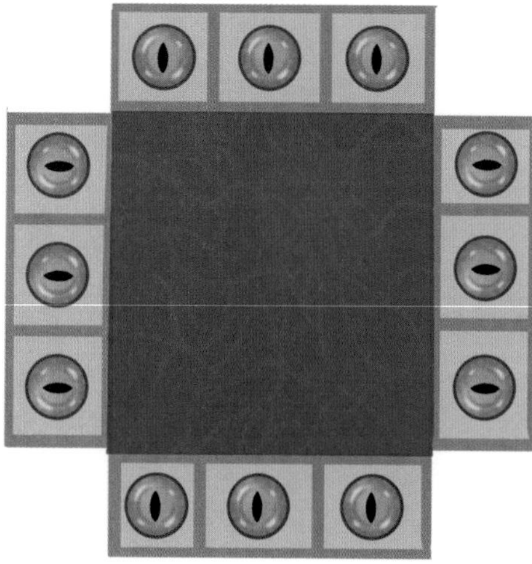

Discovering the location of an End portal is a complicated task, but it's good mental preparation for an encounter with the terrible ender dragon. . . .

#4

There is no place more hostile than the End. Jumping into the void of a portal can be terrifying for feeble creatures, but judging by your progress, that's no longer entirely true for you. So tell me which of these statements is true.

1. Once across the portal, you'll reappear on a floating section of obsidian.
2. Once across the portal, the only solution to leave to the End is to kill the ender dragon.
3. Once across the portal, you must start by avoiding the ender dragon that spawns in front of you.

NOTE YOUR NUMBER OF POINTS HERE

#5

I'll keep repeating it until it's penetrated your thick skull: whenever you explore a dangerous location, it is essential to know all of its elements. Show me which of the following blocks do not belong in the End.

1. The crimson stone block.
2. The white stone block.
3. The chest.
4. The lava block.
5. The End stone block.
6. The soul sand block.
7. The shulker box.
8. The glowstone block.
9. The water block.
10. The magma block.
11. The dirt block.
12. The stone block.

#6

Among the following items, which one will make your life easier in the End?

1. A pumpkin.
2. An ender pearl.
3. A bucket of water.
4. A compass.

#7

Given its colossal scale, you might need some help to navigate the End. Do you have the slightest idea of what will happen if you create a map and try to use it?

1. It won't display anything.
2. It will display a map in gray and white.
3. It will display only the movement marker.

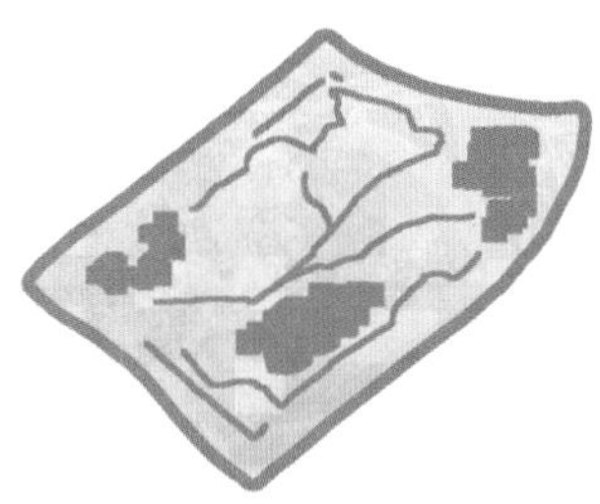

NOTE YOUR NUMBER OF POINTS HERE

Inside the End, you will find huge quantities of a new block: End stone. You can bring some back to the Overworld—if you manage to defeat the dragon. But what are the properties of End stone?

(Several answers are possible.)

1. End stone is much more resistant to explosions than normal stone.

2. The ender dragon cannot destroy End stone.

3. End stone can be picked with a tool made of any kind of material.

4. End stone is not the only block composing the End's islands.

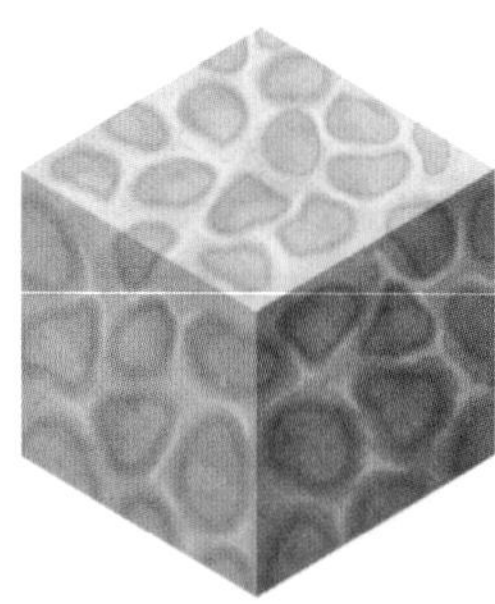

#9

If you manage to defeat the ender dragon, you'll gain new opportunities for exploration. The death of that magnificent beast will create gateway portals leading to the End's outer islands. Which of the following methods enables you to use these strange portals?

1. You have to mine the obsidian blocks surrounding the portal to access it.
2. You have to throw an ender pearl through the portal.
3. You need to hold the dragon egg in your hand to cross the portal.

Of course, you still need to defeat the ender dragon. . . . I wonder if you'll make it. I have my doubts.

NOTE YOUR NUMBER OF POINTS HERE

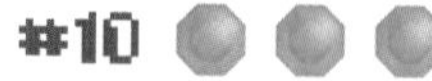

#10

Take a close look at the map below. It represents the End—and not just anyone can make sense of it. Complete the map's key to prove you won't get lost among these countless islands floating in the mortal abyss.

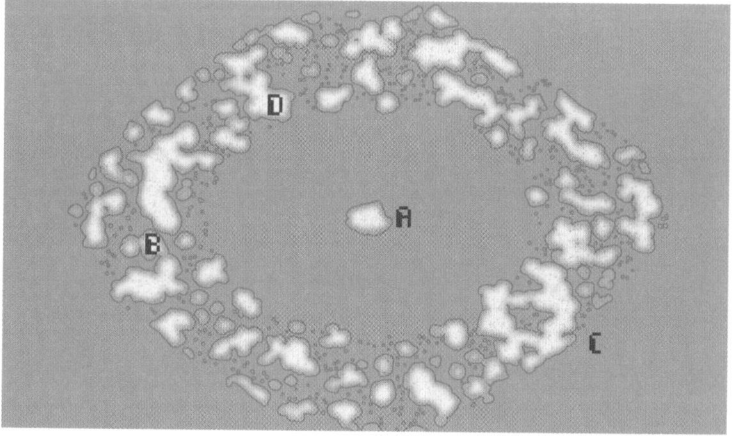

1. A: Location of the dragon battle. B: Area likely to contain End cities. C: The limits of the End. D: Area likely to contain chorus trees.
2. A: Location of the dragon battle. B: Area likely to contain End cities. C: The limits of the End. D: Location where the character spawns.
3. A: Location of the dragon battle. B: Area likely to contain exit portals. C: The limits of the End. D: Area likely to contain End cities.

Long ago, I chose to go into exile in the End to probe the darkest recesses of my soul. You can barely feel the Source out there, which is very unsettling for those accustomed to being constantly connected to it. By contemplating the nothingness around me, the power of the void eventually morphed my eyes, which started to glow like those of endermen.

#11 

End cities are full of treasures. You can even find, inside an item frame, a new way of moving around: elytra. Do you know where they're located?

1. In the End ship.
2. In the great treasure room.
3. In the banner room.
4. In the great tower.

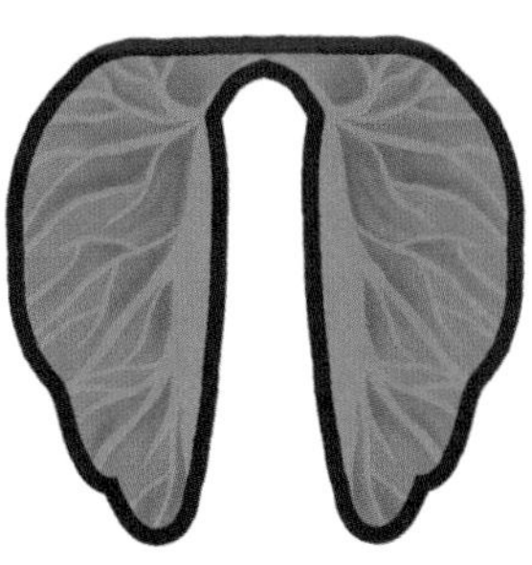

NOTE YOUR NUMBER OF POINTS HERE

#12  

Elytra enable you to glide when jumping from a certain height. If they're not enchanted with Unbreaking, do you know how far you can travel without breaking them?

1. Five thousand blocks.
2. Eight thousand blocks.
3. Thirteen thousand blocks.

As you know, flying is one of my many powers. You'll see—it's an incredible feeling.

#13 

When the ender dragon dies, an egg will appear just above the exit portal, on an obsidian pillar. If you try to pick it up, the egg will teleport away, like an enderman. Do you know how to get your hands on that trophy?

1. You need to push it with a piston block.
2. You have to gather it with the Silk Touch enchantment.
3. You have to make the egg fall on a redstone torch.

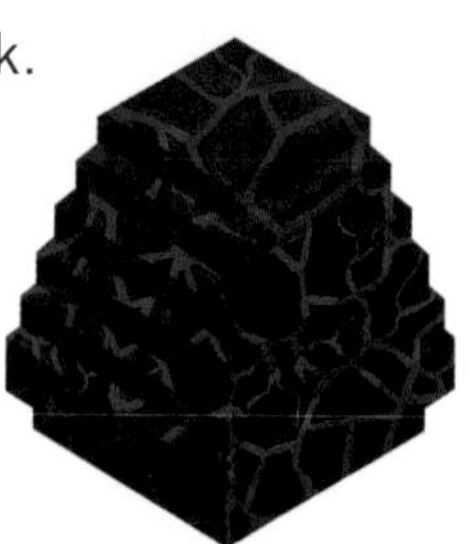

#14

Eternally I move.

I am the source of life.

From the heights I behold.

To fight the dragon,

Destroy me you must.

What am I?

NOTE YOUR NUMBER OF POINTS HERE

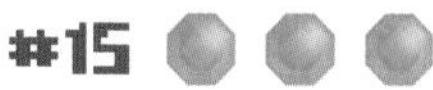

Before you go any further, let's check everything you've learned so far. To do so, complete the grid below with the corresponding words.

```
. . . . . . P . . . . . . . . . . . . . . .
. . . . . . _ . . . . . . . . . . . . . . .
. . . C _ O _ U S . . . . . . . . . . . . .
. . . . . . _ . . . . . . . . . . . . . . .
. . . . S _ _ L K _ _ . . . . . . . . . . .
. . . . . . R . . N . . B . . . . . . . . .
. . . . . . S . . D . . R . . . . _ . . . .
. . . . . . _ . . _ N _ _ R M I _ E . . . .
. . . . . . O . . _ . . W . . _ . D . . . .
_ _ _ P K _ N . . D . . _ . . L . R . . . .
. . . . . . _ . . R . . N . . _ . _ . . . .
. . . . . . . . . _ . . G . . N . _ . . . .
. . . . . . . . . _ . . _ . . D . K . . . .
. . . . . . . . . O . . _ . . . . . . . . .
. . E _ D _ _ M A _ . . _ . . . . . . . . .
. . . . . . . . . . . . N . . . . . . . . .
. . . . . . . . . . E _ D _ R _ R Y _ _ A L
```

NOTE YOUR NUMBER OF POINTS HERE

I hope you haven't forgotten the reason you're in the middle of the End. Here, and only here, will the Endercube open. But while location is one thing, you must also attain the required level to break through its final barrier.

To maintain your steady progress, you should be ready for level 11. That means you'll need at least 15 experience points earned during this exploration trial.

Your number of points is: ☐

To pass on to the building trial, you must have:

15 points.

THE BUILDING TRIAL

Roaming the End for countless years has allowed me to achieve an unrivaled mastery in the art of building. The random islands suspended in the void are a great source of inspiration! End cities are fascinating as well. Their structures and shulker-based defense systems helped me devise better protections for my own fortresses. How about you? Are you as inspired as I am by the abyss?

#1

Let's start with a trick to connect the Overworld and the End: ender chests. I hope you know how they work—their contents are shared between all chests of the same type. That makes it possible to stash resources in the End. Complete the crafting table below to create such a chest.

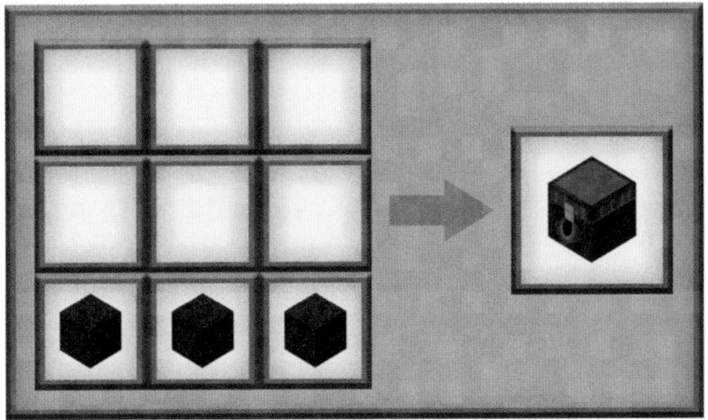

Feel like you're being watched by the green eye of the chest? Don't worry, it's perfectly normal. It wouldn't take much for me to get attached to this little cyclopean guy.

NOTE YOUR NUMBER OF POINTS HERE

#2 

In addition to the previous point, what's one other special feature of ender chests?

1. The ender chest has thirty-six storage slots instead of the usual twenty-seven.
2. The ender chest is impervious to explosions.
3. The ender chest can connect the Overworld and the End, but not the Nether and the End.

#3  

There are unique materials in the End, with shades of color that can't be found anywhere else. For instance, the purple rock called "purpur block" constitutes the majority of End cities. It takes several steps to create, starting by smelting a specific ingredient. Which one?

#4

I understand how creepy the End's void may seem to you. Personally, I think it lets me refocus and channel my anger into better plans. Anyway, you can break up the monotony of this place with a jukebox, at least if you have music discs! From the list below, which surprising trick produces such a disc?

1. You can get a disc when a creeper is killed by a skeleton's arrow.
2. You can get a disc when an enderman is struck by lightning.
3. You can get a disc by using a shovel to inflict the fatal strike to the ender dragon.

"Aria Math" is the best song ever, hands down!

NOTE YOUR NUMBER OF POINTS HERE

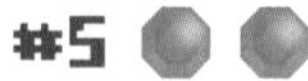

#5

If you wish to please me—and you should—I suggest you build a structure similar to an End city near your base in the Overworld. As you know, I just love this kind of architecture. Among these blocks, which ones would be useless for constructing such a building?

1. A block of purpur stone.
2. A block of white stone.
3. A block of chiseled purpur stone.
4. A block of End stone.
5. A block of pink wool.

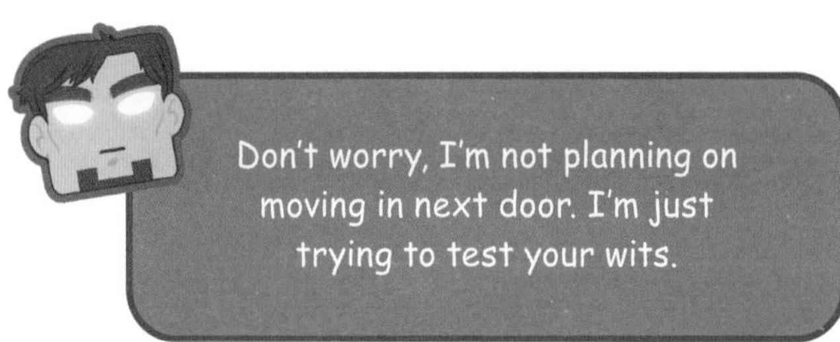

#6

In the End, there are new and interesting ways of stocking your loot. We already covered the ender chest, but there's also the shulker box, named after the infamous shell monster. Complete the crafting table below, and pick the best description of this object.

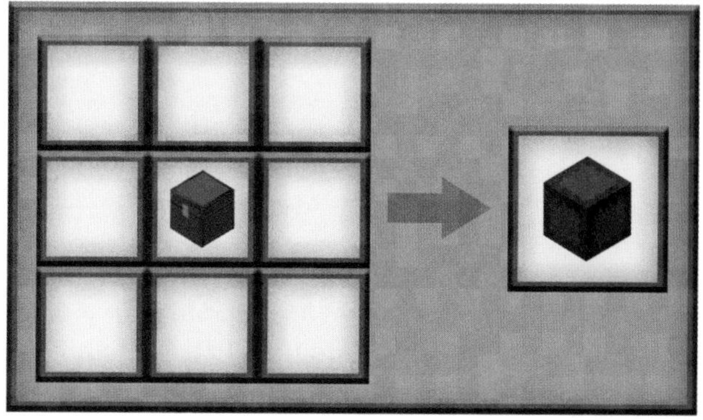

1. The shulker box's color changes automatically depending on its environment.
2. The shulker box preserves its content when it's broken.
3. The shulker box can defend itself when hostile creatures are nearby.

NOTE YOUR NUMBER OF POINTS HERE

At first, I wanted to keep the Endercube inside a shulker box. Unfortunately, the cube absorbed every particle of it. I decided to keep it with me at all times, because if I left it alone, it could annihilate the entire world and I wouldn't even get to watch. It's not particularly burdensome, but lately its inner power seems ready to explode.

Until now, I've asked you what you could craft with a specific inventory or what was missing to create an object. I'm going to spice things up a little bit and ask you to give me the full list of required items to craft one map, two armor stands, and one rabbit stew.

More resilient and also more pleasing to the eye, chiseled blocks are a common sight in Minecraft. One of the answers below lists all types. Which one?

1. Chiseled stone, chiseled mossy stone, and chiseled purpur block.
2. Chiseled stone, chiseled purpur block, and chiseled quartz.
3. Chiseled stone, chiseled purpur block, and chiseled bricks.

#9 

One of the following objects does not require redstone to work. Which one?

1. A dispenser.
2. A dropper.
3. A beacon.
4. A note block.

NOTE YOUR NUMBER OF POINTS HERE

#10

In End cities, you'll encounter a new light source: End rods. Thanks to their peculiar shape, your home will have a real "ender look." Can you tell which other object produces the same amount of light?

1. A magma block.
2. A furnace.
3. A redstone torch.
4. A torch.

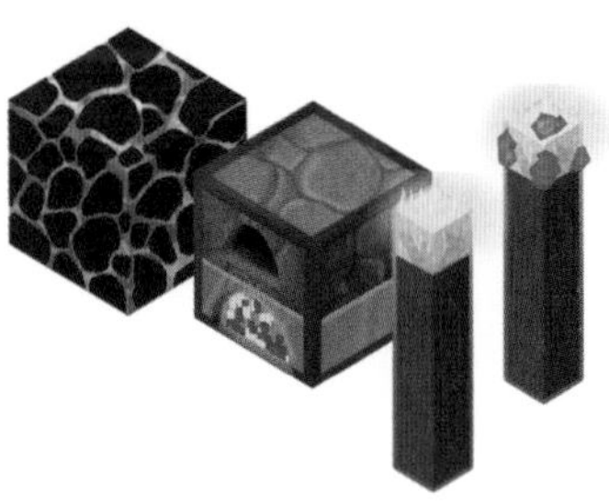

#11

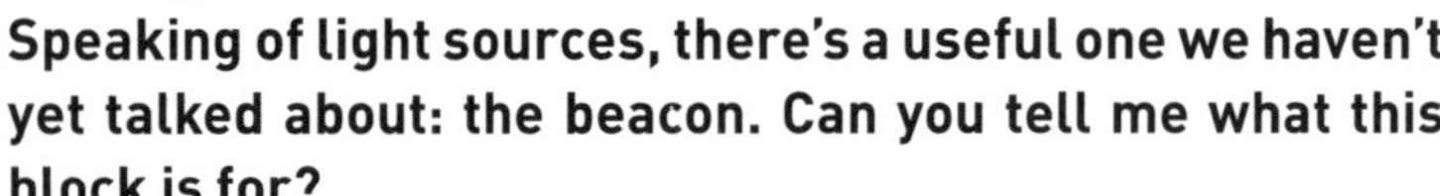

Speaking of light sources, there's a useful one we haven't yet talked about: the beacon. Can you tell me what this block is for?

1. The beacon projects a light beam skyward, visible from far away, and provides status effects to the player.
2. The beacon projects a light beam skyward, visible from far away, and can be used as a teleporter if activated correctly.
3. The beacon projects a light beam skyward, visible from far away, and is also a save point, like a bed.

#12 

Here's a question to test your curiosity. What happens when you pour water on an End crystal?

1. The crystal will break and can't be picked up.
2. Water will change to ice, protecting the crystal inside.
3. It creates an infinite loop of combusting and extinguishing.

NOTE YOUR NUMBER OF POINTS HERE

#13

It is normally impossible to have two chests side by side, as they automatically merge to create one big chest. Do you know the trick to get the same result as in this picture?

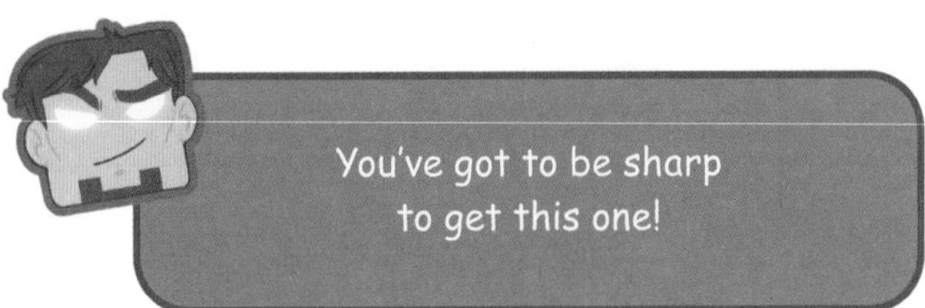

Dyes allow you to customize many items, but you need to know how to collect them first.

Match the colors below with the elements that produce them.

1. Lilac.
2. Poppy.
3. Sunflower.
4. Ink sac.
5. Cocoa beans.
6. Peony.
7. Oxeye daisy.
8. Lapis lazuli.

A. Magenta.
B. Light gray.
C. Yellow.
D. Pink.
E. Blue.
F. Black.
G. Brown.
H. Red.

NOTE YOUR NUMBER OF POINTS HERE

#15 

Once the ender dragon is vanquished, a portal leading back to the Overworld will appear just below the pillar where the dragon egg is stored. What will happen if you place four End crystals around this portal?

1. The portal will activate.

2. The ender dragon will be revived.

3. The portal's destination will change.

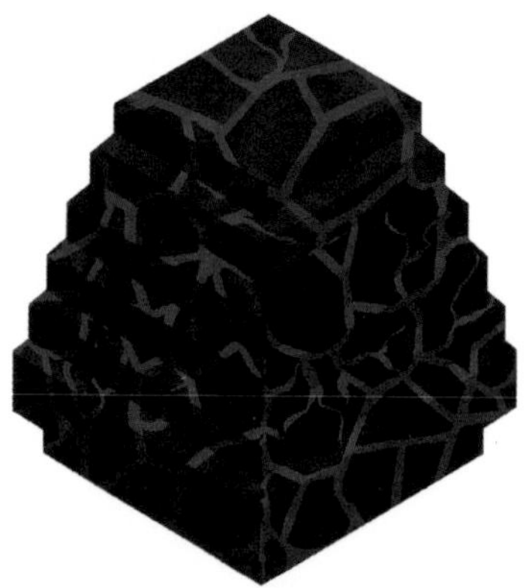

NOTE YOUR NUMBER OF POINTS HERE

I'm sure you've never been so close to success in your entire life. Actually, you have only three trials left before the final puzzle of the Endercube. Don't lower your guard yet; the only way to make it to the end is to stay focused.

You think you're good for level 12? I hope so, but you need at least 35 experience points.

Your number of points is: ☐

In order to proceed to the farming trial, you need a minimum of:

35 points.

THE FARMING TRIAL

The Endercube is an incredible source of knowledge and power, but it won't provide any kind of sustenance. To travel in the End, you'll need a stockpile of high-quality food supplies. And if you have enough patience to grow your own crops, the experience might even bring you . . . well . . . you know, that strange thingy? What's the name again . . . happiness? Does that ring any bells? It doesn't for me, but I'm pretty sure that's it.

#1

In order to save some time and enjoy your trips in parallel worlds, I'll remind you again how important it is to automate your crops. Pistons are essential for this: they can destroy your crop blocks, meaning all you have to do is gather the goodies! There are two types of pistons, normal and sticky. Do you know how to create them with a crafting table?

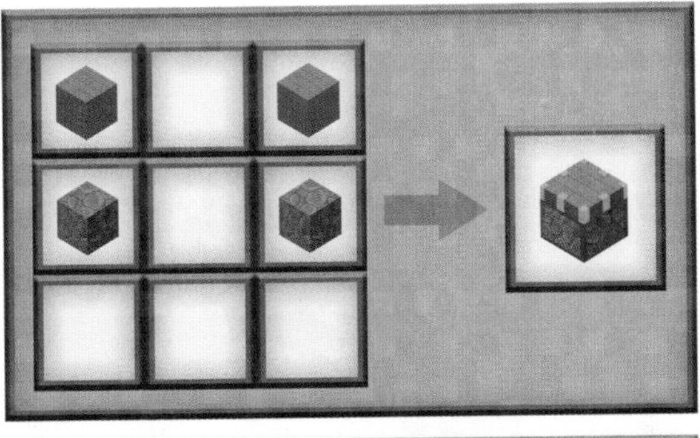

Of course, I strongly advise you to pair your piston system with a crop-harvesting system.

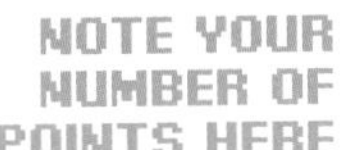

#2

Minecraft is full of surprising places. One of them in particular made a lasting impression on me when I discovered it. It's a fantastic place and full of possibilities for someone who likes plants and farming. Do you know which one I'm talking about?

1. The mushroom island.
2. The lilac mountain.
3. The orchid crater.

There is an animal we haven't discussed yet: the ocelot. You can tame it and it will become your pet cat. From the following methods, pick the most effective.

1. You have to hold a fish in your hand to attract the ocelot, wait for it to sit down, give it the fish, and repeat until it's tamed.
2. You have to stay a few blocks away from the ocelot, wait for it to come and ask for food, give it fish, and repeat until it's tamed.
3. You have to approach the ocelot slowly so as not to scare it, wait for it to ask for food, give it fish, then use a leash.

NOTE YOUR NUMBER OF POINTS HERE

Once inside your house with your new cat, you'd better order it to sit somewhere. Why is that?

1. Otherwise, it will wander in the house and steal food when it's hungry.
2. Otherwise, it will open doors by jumping on them and wander away to dangerous places.
3. Otherwise, it will try to sit on blocks, like furnaces, preventing you from using them.

What an unbearable animal! What kind of moron would fall in love with these pests?

#5

We've already covered trees in previous trials, so you know there are many different types. I'd like you to match each wood block below to its corresponding name. Believe me, it's easier said than done. . . .

1. Dark oak.
2. Birch.
3. Oak.
4. Jungle.
5. Acacia.

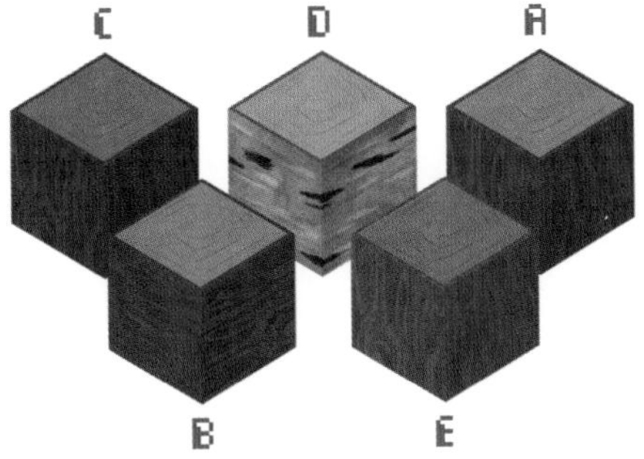

NOTE YOUR NUMBER OF POINTS HERE

Peaceful animals look so cute . . . which makes it all the more fun to chop them up for food. If you enchant your sword with "Fire Aspect," it will have a specific effect on such animals. What will it do?

1. Animals killed with this weapon will drop coal instead of meat.
2. Animals killed with this weapon will drop twice the amount of meat.
3. Animals killed with this weapon will drop cooked meat.

#7

You're in a tricky spot. You have to gather all the seeds in the illustration below, but you need to eat every three steps. Since you can't eat the seeds, you can't step on them for your third movement. Watch out for the monsters: they'll pulverize you if you pass within a block of them. Can you find the right path?

(You can't move diagonally.)

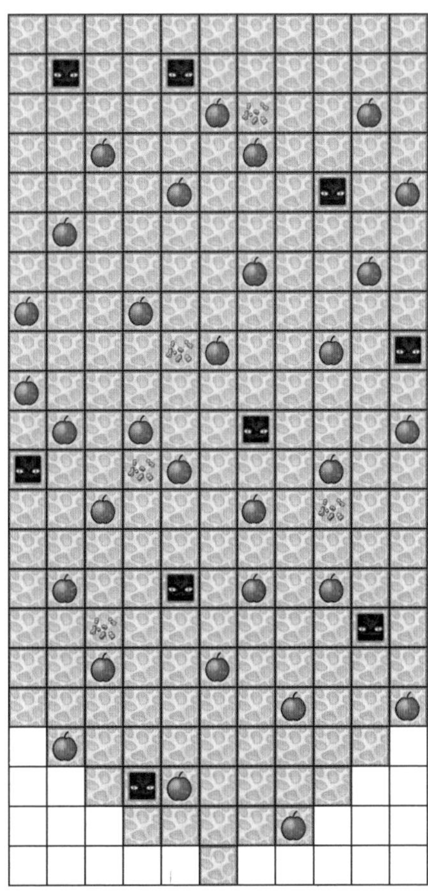

NOTE YOUR NUMBER OF POINTS HERE

If you were hoping to find heaps of plants in the End, forget about it. The void is not the best place to grow crops. The only plants you'll find are chorus trees, which may yield chorus fruit. What will happen if you decide to cut the trunk of this strange tree?

1. Nothing. You have to harvest the fruit from high up.
2. All of the other blocks of the plant will be destroyed.
3. Only the block you hit will be destroyed; the rest of the plant will remain intact.

#9

You can eat the chorus fruit. Its peculiar taste is unforgettable. After what happened the first time I tried it, it took me a while to eat it again. Something strange occurs when you eat a chorus fruit—what is it?

1. Purple sparks fly around you, and you start to levitate.
2. You're teleported like an enderman, and then purple sparks fly around you.
3. Purple sparks fly around you, then it hurts you and inflicts the "Poison" status.

Not so obvious, is it? Did I overestimate you this time?

NOTE YOUR NUMBER OF POINTS HERE

Remember when you found a cookie earlier while solving a riddle? The funniest thing happened. . . . I can't find it in my inventory anymore. If you really want to earn my legacy, you absolutely must know how to craft them. Complete the crafting table below, and tell me how many cookies this will produce.

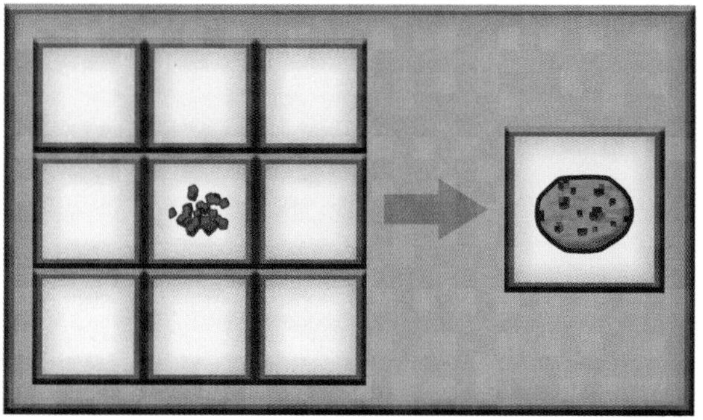

1. Four cookies.
2. Six cookies.
3. Eight cookies.

Speaking of cookies—as you can see, cocoa beans are an essential ingredient. You can find them in cocoa pods. How do you grow them?

1. They need to grow vertically, to a height of at least three blocks.
2. They can grow on any type of wood, as long as it's irrigated.
3. They need to grow vertically on jungle wood.

NOTE YOUR NUMBER OF POINTS HERE

#12 

You may not know this, but it's possible to plant seeds from the Overworld in the End. But there's one small problem. What is it?

1. The plants will take twice as much time to grow.
2. The plants will never grow.
3. The plants will need a source of light, like a glowstone.

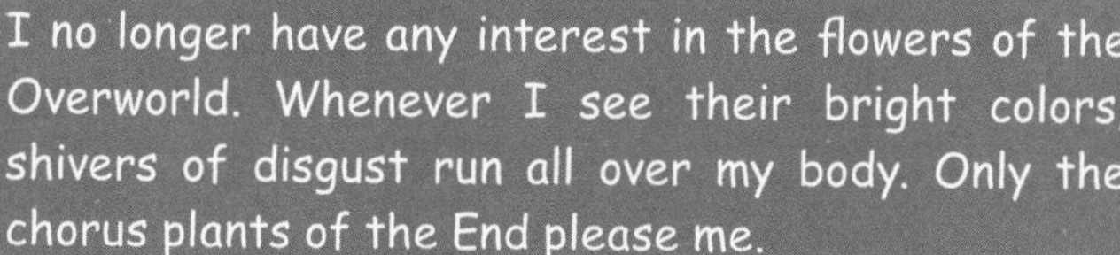

#13

From the End, I take my name.

Rarely can I be found.

Teleportation creates me.

I disappear in the blink of an eye.

What am I?

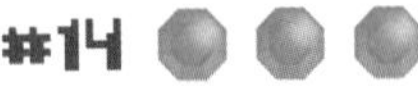

As I've already said, bone meal is incredibly useful for speeding up growth. Unfortunately, it doesn't work for every plant. In the list of plants below, mark the ones on which bone meal has no effect.

1. Cactus.
2. Mushroom.
3. Pumpkin.
4. Tree sap.
5. Nether wart.
6. Melon.
7. Chorus plant.

NOTE YOUR NUMBER OF POINTS HERE

#15 

It's an extremely bad idea to create a pig farm in a jungle biome. Why is that?

1. The ocelots in the jungle are likely to attack the pigs.
2. Pig breeding in the jungle is harder because of the environment.
3. Lightning strikes more often in the jungle biome, which can turn pigs into zombie pigmen.

NOTE YOUR NUMBER OF POINTS HERE

It looks like you know enough about farming to survive easily. I spotted a few mistakes here and there but nothing serious. After all, nobody's perfect . . . except me. The mining trial might be nothing more than a formality for you. But after this, you will face the ender dragon. . . .

Let's count the experience you gained and see if you can move on to level 13.

Do you have the mandatory 55 points?

Your number of points is:

In order to continue to the mining trial, you must have at least:

55 points.

THE MINING TRIAL

"Mining in the End?" I know it sounds strange, since digging too far in this world means falling into the abyss. But that doesn't mean you get to forget how to mine the Overworld! Should you ever fall to your death in the End, you'll lose all your equipment. And that means you can never have too many diamonds stockpiled in your chests. So pull out your pickaxe and get ready!

#1

You're already aware that Minecraft's ores are spread out over several layers, so now I have a tougher challenge for you. Match each ore below with the range of layers in which you can find them.

1. Coal.	**A.** 0 to 130.
2. Diamond.	**B.** 0 to 32.
3. Emerald.	**C.** 0 to 15.
4. Iron.	**D.** 0 to 32.
5. Lapis lazuli.	**E.** 0 to 64.
6. Gold.	**F.** 0 to 15.
7. Redstone.	**G.** 0 to 30.

NOTE YOUR NUMBER OF POINTS HERE

#2

I just realized I haven't quizzed you about dungeons yet. You've probably found one of these lovely places while mining the Overworld. They're always full of mob spawners. Of the following statements, only one is true. Which one?

1. In order to turn off a mob spawner, you must place a torch on all of its faces.
2. In order to turn off a mob spawner, you must cover it with any block.
3. In order to turn off a mob spawner, you must place torches everywhere in the dungeon and all around the spawner block.

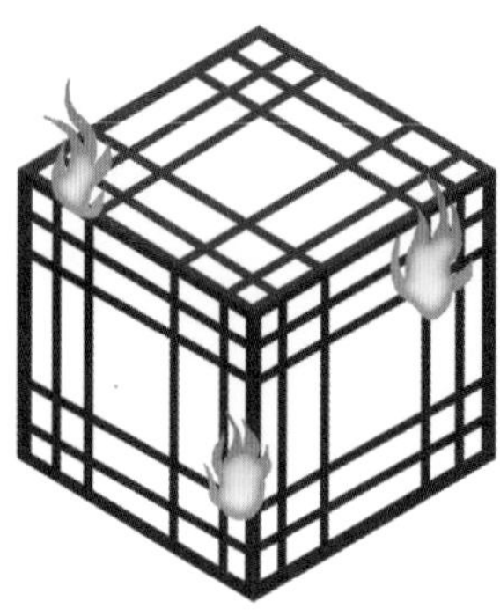

#3

The Fortune enchantment is essential for mining jobs. It allows you to collect far more resources than with a non-enchanted tool. When mining a diamond ore block with the "Fortune III" enchantment, what is the maximum number of diamonds you can get?

1. Three diamonds.
2. Four diamonds.
3. Six diamonds.

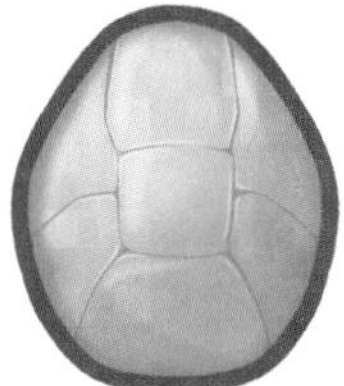

#4

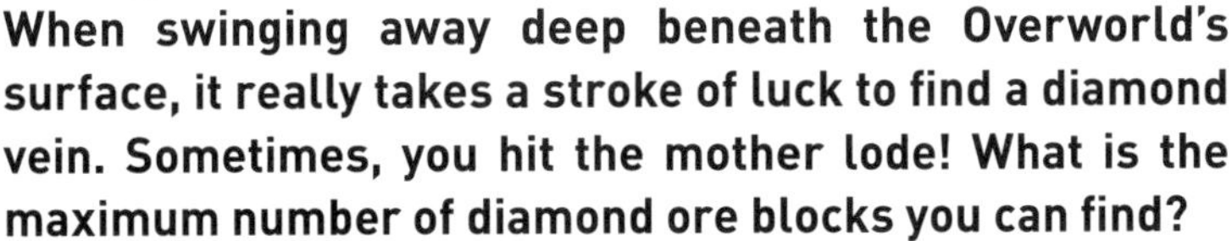

When swinging away deep beneath the Overworld's surface, it really takes a stroke of luck to find a diamond vein. Sometimes, you hit the mother lode! What is the maximum number of diamond ore blocks you can find?

1. Six diamond ore blocks.
2. Eight diamond ore blocks.
3. Twelve diamond ore blocks.

NOTE YOUR NUMBER OF POINTS HERE

#5 

We've covered the different types of minecarts, including the minecart with hopper. Remember that it has the special quality of absorbing the elements of the containers above it. But you need to start by building a hopper. Complete the crafting table below.

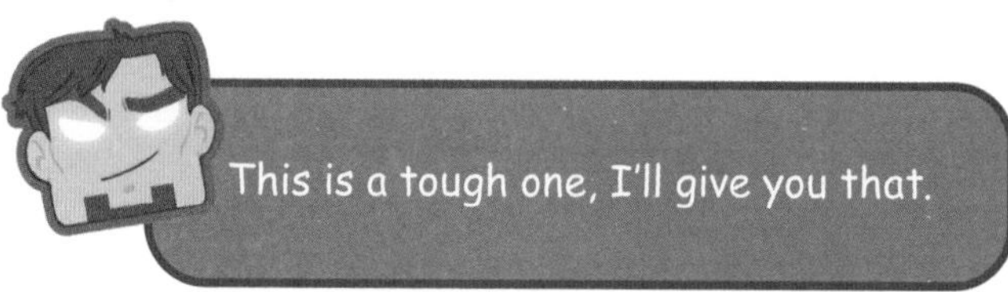

Once you reach a certain level of knowledge and practice, you want everything to go as quickly and smoothly as possible. The "Efficiency" enchantment is your friend: it allows you to mine much faster. The maximum level of this enchantment is V. Do you know how much each level increases mining speed?

1. 15% faster than the previous level.
2. 30% faster than the previous level.
3. 50% faster than the previous level.

Ladders are very useful when mining down. You can go very deep in a few seconds. What will happen if you try to eat something while climbing a ladder?

1. You'll stop moving up or down for the time it takes to eat.
2. It will take longer to eat.
3. Nothing happens.

NOTE YOUR NUMBER OF POINTS HERE

According to you, what is the strength of a TNT explosion compared to a creeper explosion?

1. The explosion is the same.
2. The TNT explosion is stronger than the creeper explosion.
3. The creeper explosion is stronger than the TNT explosion.

Among the following objects, which cannot activate a TNT block?

(Several answers are possible.)

1. A bucket of lava.
2. A single repeater.
3. A damage potion.
4. Flint and steel.
5. A redstone torch.

Every once in a while, I still love placing a few TNT blocks here and there. Well, all right, a LOT of blocks. And everywhere. Then I activate them all, just for fun. BOOOM! Don't act like you haven't done the same thing!

NOTE YOUR NUMBER OF POINTS HERE

#10   

It's been a while since I created a little role-playing exercise for you. Let's say you want to upgrade your underground base. Here's what's in your chest. With the chest's contents, as well as what's in your inventory, what can you craft?

Chest:

Inventory:

1. One diamond pickaxe, two chests, twelve ladders, one TNT, one minecart with hopper, and eight stairs.
2. Two diamond shovels, one iron sword, twenty ladders, one chest, one TNT minecart, and twenty stairs.
3. Two iron pickaxes, one diamond sword, fifteen ladders, one TNT, one minecart with hopper, and twelve stairs.

Thanks to my exile in the depths of the End, I learned how to count everything, anticipate everything, and optimize everything. Even under the greatest pressure and the threat of danger, I can visualize all crafting possibilities with what I have at hand and in my inventory. Contact with the void opened my mind to the Source and allowed me to design the Endercube and much more.

#11

Can you tell me how to spot a stone infested with silverfish?

1. The stone block is slightly darker.
2. Stone particles fall from the block.
3. You can easily destroy the block by hand.
4. When listening carefully, you can hear the silverfish.

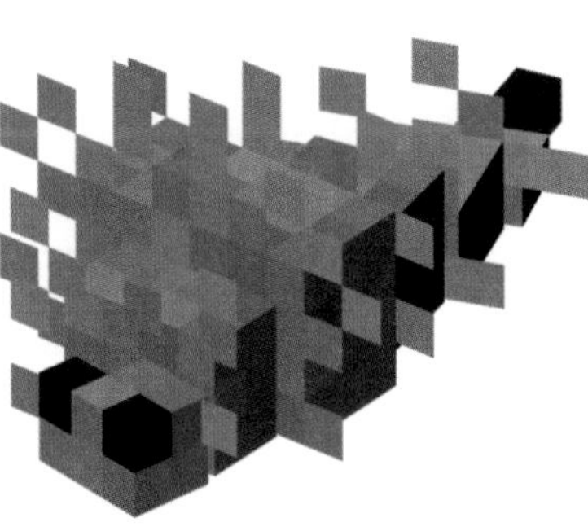

NOTE YOUR NUMBER OF POINTS HERE

For this one, you have to be attentive and closely observe the image below. As you can see, there are several missing elements. You need to complete this grid, filling in the empty spaces so that each type of block only appears once in each row, column, and diagonal line.

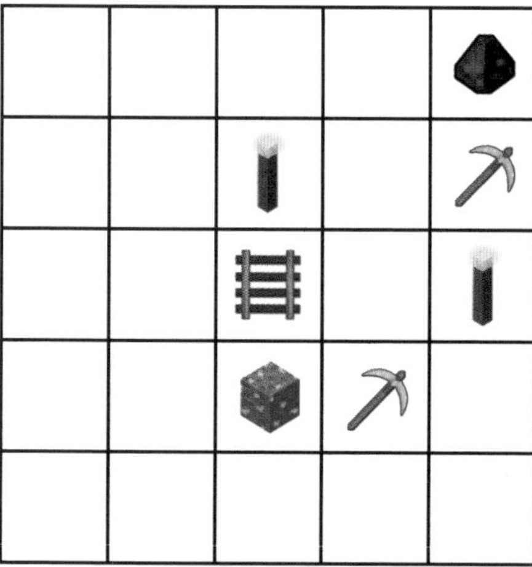

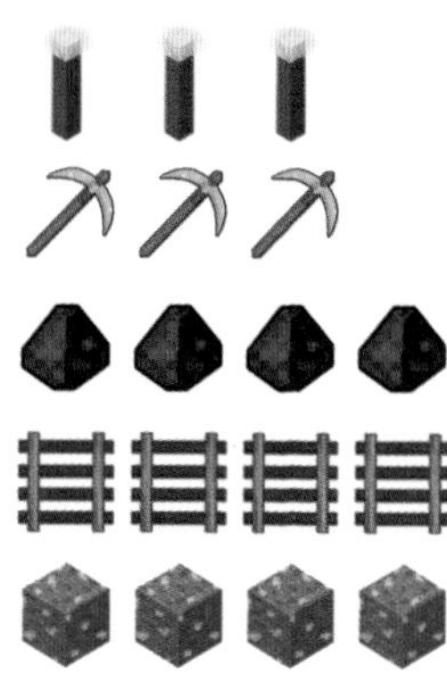

I've spent many hours of my life playing this game. . . .

#13 

You can have a lot of fun inside a minecart. Long rail trips can even be a good opportunity to meditate. But you need to design a railway that can propel a cart. How far can a section of powered rails propel a loaded minecart?

1. Forty-six blocks.
2. Fifty-two blocks.
3. Sixty-four blocks.

#14

I hope you're the type of adventurer who plans ahead. You might want to craft a potion of Night Vision in case you run out of torches deep inside a mine. What should you add to an Awkward potion to do so?

1. A golden carrot.
2. A spider eye.
3. A ghast tear.
4. A glistering melon slice.

NOTE YOUR NUMBER OF POINTS HERE

#15 

Take a look at this specific setup. I think I know what's going to happen. How about you?

1. The minecart will get stuck and won't be able to go up or down.
2. The minecart will be able to go down the slope but not up.
3. The minecart won't be able to go down the slope, but it will be able to go up it.

NOTE YOUR NUMBER OF POINTS HERE

It's hard to believe the fact that you aren't currently rotting in the dark and distant corners of an abandoned mine. . . . You're full of surprises! If only I could still be surprised by anything. . . . Anyway, you have yet to undergo the combat trial. And believe me, I'm a nice guy compared to the ender dragon.

Before proving you're up to the task, let's calculate your experience points. You'll need to be at least level 14 (i.e., have 80 experience points) before facing the dragon's wrath. If you're not there yet, continue your training and visit the End a few more times.

Your number of points is:

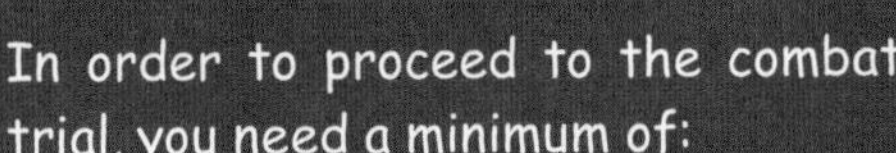

In order to proceed to the combat trial, you need a minimum of:

80 points.

THE COMBAT TRIAL

I remember the first time I set foot in the End and heard the dragon's roar. Its powerful growl vibrated through my body and echoed off the suspended islands before ringing out into the infinite void. When my new eyes fell upon the flying beast, I was stunned by its destructive grace. My fight against the dragon was memorable. I may tell you about it one day, but for now it's your turn to face it.

#1 

Sometimes before a fight, you need to relax and sharpen your mind at the same time. Here is one of my favorite games. I dubbed it "Dominocraft," but you can call it whatever you want. The goal is to find the right placements for the missing pieces.

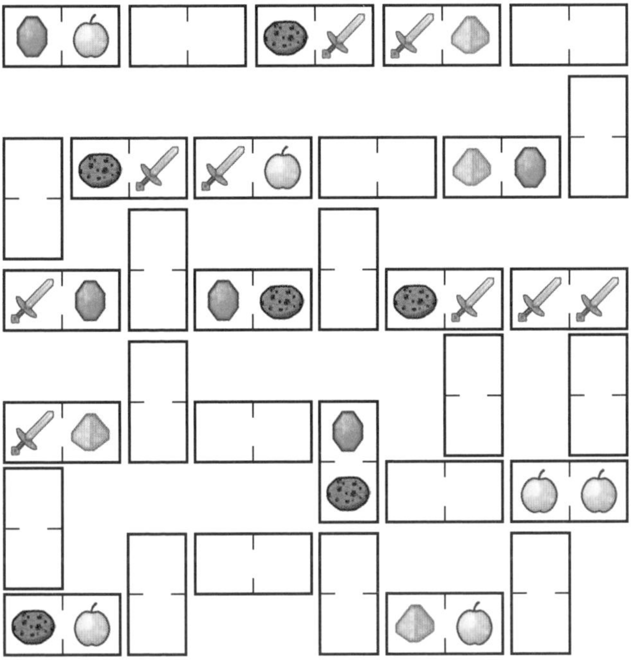

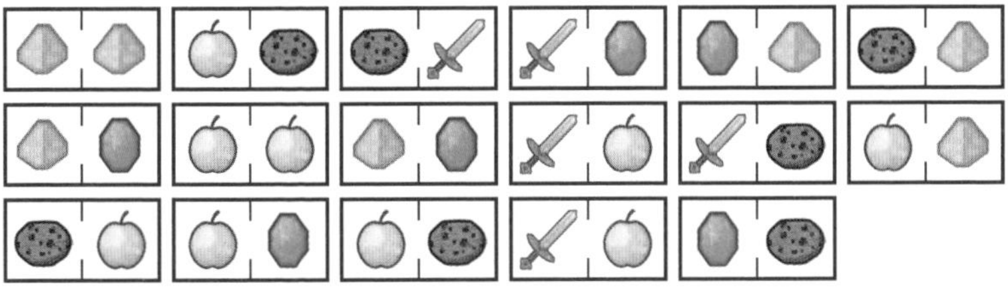

NOTE YOUR NUMBER OF POINTS HERE

If an enderman is hit by a dragon attack, what will happen?

1. It will become hostile toward the dragon.
2. It will become hostile toward you.
3. It will do nothing.

#3

It's a good idea to destroy the End crystals while they are healing the ender dragon. Do you know why?

1. It will freeze the dragon for a little while.
2. It will deal damage to the dragon.
3. It will destroy the other crystals that are healing the dragon.

#4

Since they're perched on high pillars, destroying End crystals is a dangerous task. Fortunately, there a few tricks. Below are several items—only a few of them can easily destroy the crystals while avoiding the risk of being knocked off the pillar by the dragon. Which items are they?

1. A snowball.
2. An ender pearl.
3. A bow.
4. A splash potion.
5. A fishing rod.
6. An egg.

NOTE YOUR NUMBER OF POINTS HERE

On some pillars, the crystals are protected by iron rods, forcing you to climb to the top. Which pillars are these?

1. The two highest pillars.
2. The second-smallest pillar and the second-highest pillar.
3. The second- and third-smallest pillars.

Now that you know destroying the crystals must be your priority before facing the dragon herself, can you tell me what will happen every time you smash one of them?

1. The ender dragon will immediately attack you.
2. The resulting explosion may hurt you.
3. The endermen will stare at you.
4. Before vanishing, the crystal will send a lethal fireball in your direction.

#7

You can gather some of the dragon's breath with an empty vial when she exhales purple flames. In the brewing stand below, a vial of dragon's breath is combined with a splash potion. What will it do?

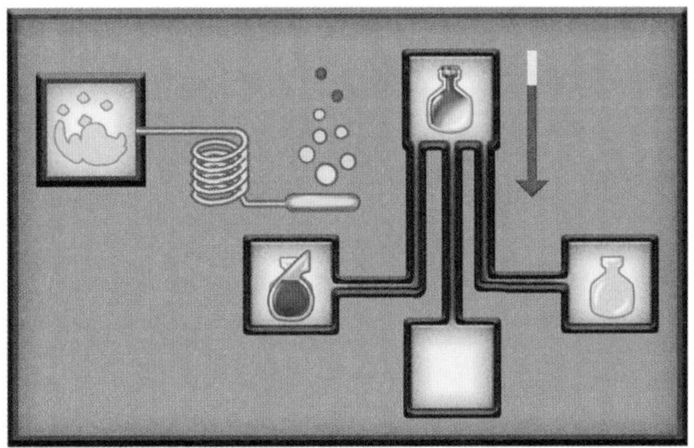

1. It will increase the potion's effects tenfold.
2. The potion will become a lingering potion.
3. It will double the potion's area of effect.

To create the mighty core of the Endercube, not only did I use ender pearls, but I also added some dragon's breath. In theory, someone else could be intelligent and adventurous enough to create an object of such complexity, but they would never be able to link it to the Source of Minecraft like I did.

NOTE YOUR NUMBER OF POINTS HERE

The fight against the ender dragon is divided into several predictable phases. I know this monster well: from a simple glance at her wings, I can guess her next move. How about you? I doubt it! At least try to tell me which of the following attacks it will never perform.

(Several answers are possible.)

1. Charging ahead to inflict damage.
2. Falling on you to deal area-of-effect damage.
3. Throwing an acid ball at you.
4. Breathing fire at you.
5. Hitting you with her tail.

The ender dragon is rushing at you. In your desperation, this is what you built. What is the purpose of such a structure?

1. To block the dragon before she gets to you.
2. None. Death is inevitable.
3. To make the dragon change course to try to avoid the wall.

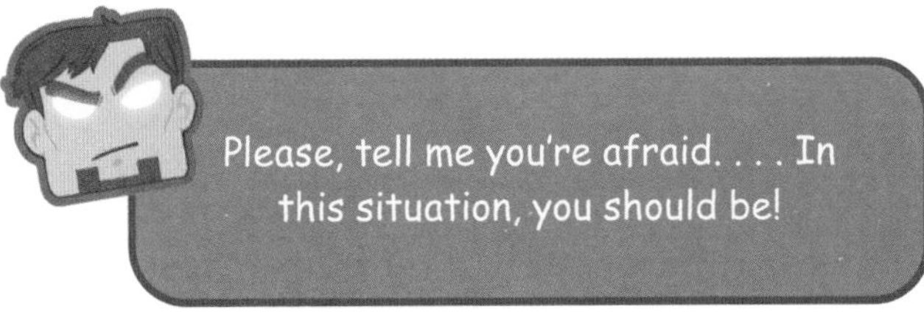

NOTE YOUR NUMBER OF POINTS HERE

We've already discussed the numerous kinds of helpful enchantments, but you'll have to be careful when you find enchanted equipment. Some items can be cursed. For instance, what does the "Curse of Binding" do?

1. Once equipped, the item can be removed, but you'll take periodic damage.
2. Once equipped, the item can't be removed unless you die.
3. Once equipped, the item can be removed, but you'll lose all XP.

#11 

Speaking of enchantments, let's study the ones that can be helpful in combat. I'd like you to associate each enchantment with its corresponding effect. As you can see, there are more effects than enchantments. This is intentional—some of them are fake, so be very careful.

1. "Sweeping Edge I."
2. "Smite I."
3. "Fire Aspect I."
4. "Knockback I."
5. "Bane of Arthropods I."
6. "Sharpness I."

A. Increases damage.
B. Inflicts Wither effect to enemies hit.
C. Increases damage only to spiders and cave spiders.
D. Increases damage to zombies, zombie pigmen, skeletons, wither skeletons, and withers.
E. Increases damage to spiders, cave spiders, silverfish, and endermites.
F. Inflicts nonpersistent fire damage to enemies.
G. Pushes back an enemy three blocks away.
H. Ignites the target and inflicts additional damage.
I. Pushes back an enemy six blocks away.
J. Increases sweeping attack damage to nearby targets.

NOTE YOUR NUMBER OF POINTS HERE

#12

The End cities are inhabited by shulkers. These monsters are very clever, which is why you often mistake them for a block of purpur. When they open their shells, they start shooting projectiles at their foes. The projectiles have a specific effect, in addition to inflicting damage. What is it?

1. Poison.
2. Levitation.
3. Slowness.
4. Weakness.

#13

When a shulker is gravely wounded, its behavior changes. What does it do?

1. It fires twice as many projectiles, twice as fast.
2. It closes down its shell for a long time.
3. It teleports.

Shulkers aren't invulnerable, but they do have quite a few qualities that protect them. From the list below, identify the items that would be completely useless against a shulker that's locked in its shell.

1. A bow.
2. A diamond sword.
3. An iron axe.
4. A splash potion of Harming.

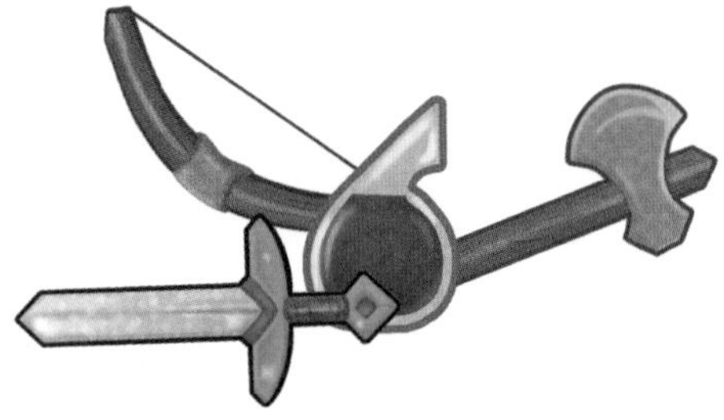

It may not look like it, but these critters are both smart and resistant. Did you know that their armor increases by 80% when they're protected by their shell?

NOTE YOUR NUMBER OF POINTS HERE

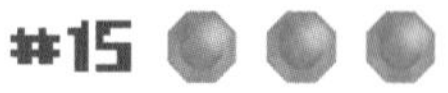

Here is one of the toughest riddles you'll face. It's sort of an investigation, and you're in charge. You need to figure out a set of specific details for each monster.

A creeper, a slime, a zombie, and an enderman are all on the outskirts of a village. They are five, six, seven, and eight years old. Each of them like a specific animal: a sheep, a pig, a cow, or a bear. Finally, they all have a favorite block: gold, diamond, wood, or obsidian.

Here is a list of the clues you need to complete the following table.

- The monster who likes gold blocks also likes pigs. It is neither the zombie nor the enderman.
- The one who likes sheep is seven years old and dislikes diamond blocks.
- The monster who likes gold blocks is eight years old and dislikes big animals.
- The slime likes wood blocks and is six years old.
- The monster who likes diamond blocks is also fond of cows.
- The enderman is allergic to wool.

Monster	Favorite animal	Favorite block	Age
Creeper			
Slime			
Zombie			
Enderman			

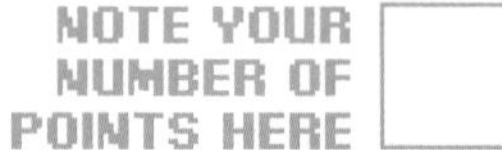

Your first fight against the ender dragon will be forever etched in your memory. I'd rather not ask you how many times you died before succeeding. I don't want to belittle you when you managed to finish the last trial of this book. You should be proud of yourself; even I'm a little proud. Unfortunately, all of this will have been for nothing if you can't solve the final riddle of the Endercube.

Before that, make sure you've reached level 15, which means 100 points overall from the expert trials.

Your number of points is: 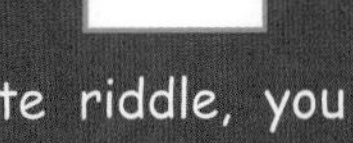

To get to the ultimate riddle, you must have:

100 points.

If that's not the case, you may try to solve the puzzle at your own risk. I've already warned you: if you're not strong enough, the cube will destroy you.

ENDERCUBE PUZZLE #3

I should warn you . . . this last challenge will give you a hard time. A word of advice: don't give up. You are so close to achieving limitless knowledge and power. Who knows, maybe you'll even sense the Source I've spoken so much about!

ENDERCUBE PUZZLE #3

To start, you need to decipher the text of each riddle. I've provided some letters to help you deduce the missing ones. Feel free to write down the letters you find in the alphabet below, so you can keep track. Once you've deciphered the text, you'll need to solve the four riddles. Each solution is one word. The final step will be discovering the thing that all four words have in common. This fifth word is the key that opens the Endercube.

EXPERT

First word:

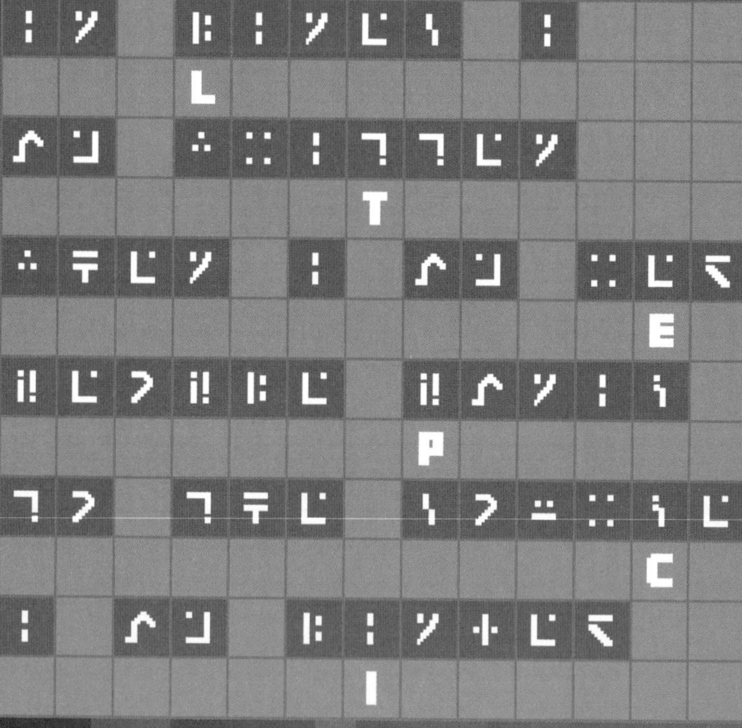

ENDERCUBE PUZZLE #3

Second word:

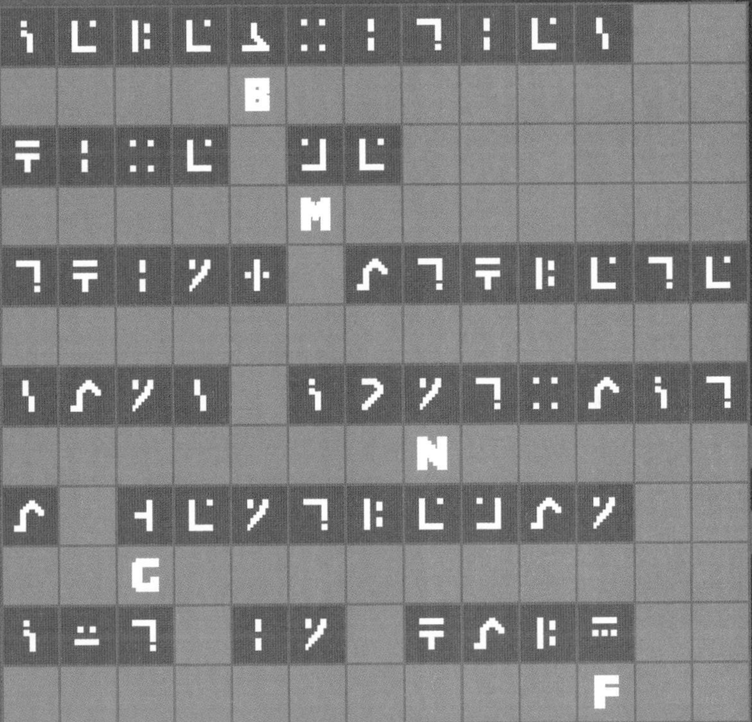

EXPERT

Third word:

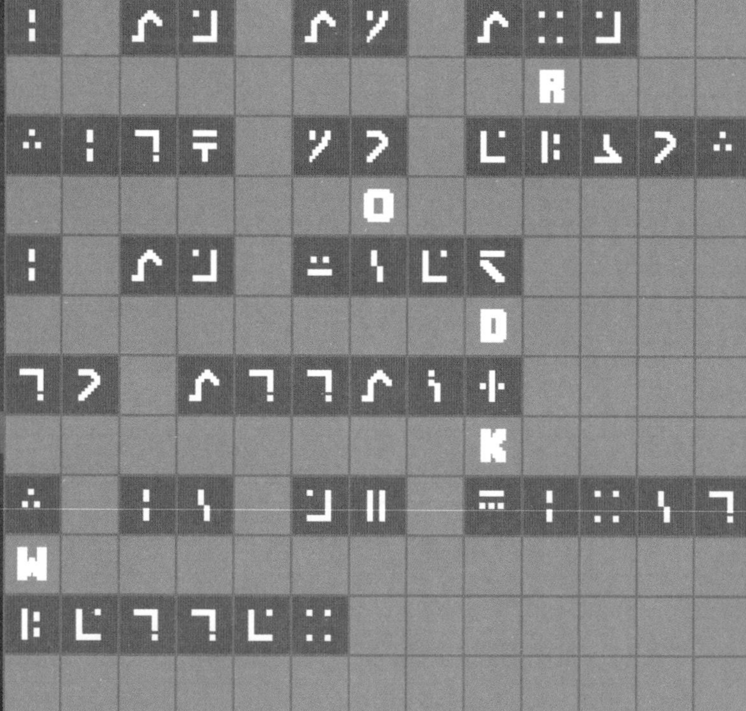

ENDERCUBE PUZZLE #3

Fourth word:

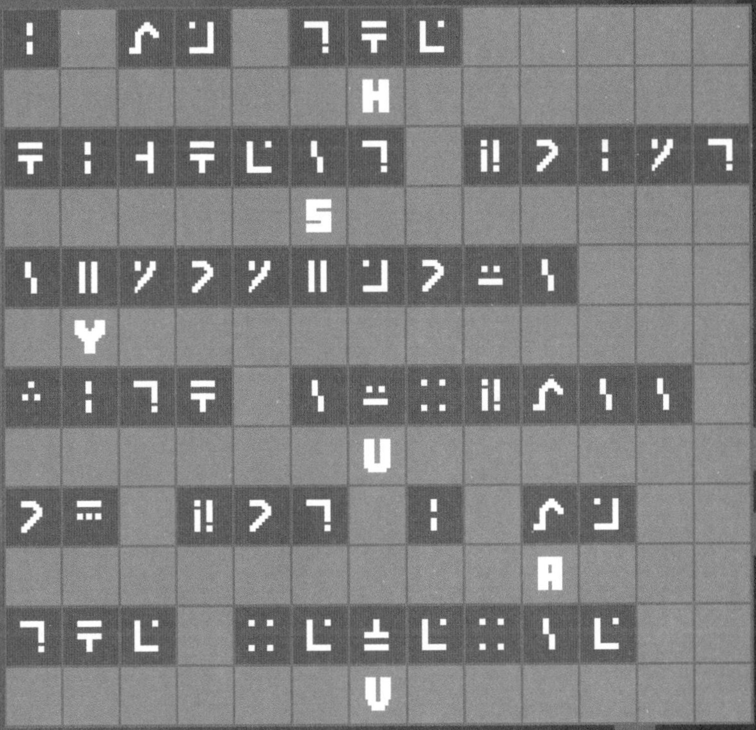

The final password is: ____________________

Have you found the key? If so, the last barrier is about to fall and reveal the ultimate truth.

I must say, when you started the novice's trials, I didn't expect you to get this far. I've been looking for someone with your skills for a long time. You can be proud of what you have accomplished. No one else had succeeded before.

Now that you're facing the truth of the Endercube, enough with the secrets! I couldn't be truthful before, since I wasn't sure of your potential. Now you must ∷ᒷᔑꖎꖎ|| know why you did all this. You ᓵᔑリリ𝙹ℸ ʖᒷᓵ𝙹ᒲᒷ ᒲ|| ⍑ᒷ╎∷, ᔑᓭ ⍑ᒷ ᔑꖎ∷ᒷᔑ↸|| ᒷ̇/╎ᓭℸᓭ. Several years ago, ╎ ᓵ∷ᒷᔑℸᒷ↸ ᔑリ 𝙹⎓⎓ᓭ!¡∷╎リ⊣ since I wanted to create a mighty power. To do so, I wielded ℸ⍑ᒷ ⍊ᒷ∷|| ᒷᓭᓭᒷリᓵᒷ 𝙹⎓ ℸ⍑ᒷ ᓭ𝙹⚍∷ᓵᒷ with the help of Glitchwitch. This way, I could create ᔑリ ╎リᓵ∷ᒷ↸╎ʖꖎᒷ ʖᒷ╎リ⊣ !¡𝙹ᓭᓭᒷᓭᓭ╎リ⊣ powers and skills superior to mine.

I had started to ℸ∷ᔑ╎リ ⍑╎ᒲ so that he ʖᒷᓵᔑᒲᒷ ꖎ╎ꖌᒷ ᒲᒷ. Unfortunately, things didn't go as planned, and ℸ⍑╎ᓭ ᓭ𝙹リ, ℸ⍑╎ᓭ ⍑ᒷ╎∷—call it what you want—∷ᔑリ ᔑ∴ᔑ||.

ENDERCUBE PUZZLE #3

Although ⍑ᒷ ↸𝙹ᒷᓭ リ𝙹ℸ ᒲᔑᓭℸᒷ∷ ⍑╎ᓭ full potential, ⍑ᒷ ⍑ᔑᓭ ⎓𝙹⚍リ↸ ᔑ ∴ᔑ|| to cover ⍑╎ᓭ tracks, and I don't know ∴⍑ᒷ∷ᒷ ⍑ᒷ ╎ᓭ. As soon as ╎ ⊣𝙹 ꖎ𝙹𝙹ꖌ╎リ⊣ ⎓𝙹∷ ⍑╎ᒲ, the link between us warns ⍑╎ᒲ 𝙹⎓ ᒲ|| ᔑ!¡!¡∷𝙹ᔑᓵ⍑.

Only you can ⍑ᒷꖎ!¡ ᒲᒷ ⎓╎リ↸ ⍑╎ᒲ, as you do not have ℸ⍑╎ᓭ ᓵ𝙹リリᒷᓵℸ╎𝙹リ. That's the reason you've gone through all of these trials. You don't have a choice, since we've been linked from the moment you opened this book. Moreover, ⍑╎ᓭ power is such ℸ⍑ᔑℸ ⍑ᒷ !¡𝙹ᓭᒷᓭ ᔑ ᓭᒷ∷╎𝙹⚍ᓭ ℸ⍑∷ᒷᔑℸ ℸ𝙹 ℸ⍑ᒷ ʖᔑꖎᔑリᓵᒷ 𝙹⎓ ᒲ╎リᒷᓵ∷ᔑ⎓ℸ ᔑリ↸ ℸ𝙹 ⍑╎ᒲᓭᒷꖎ⎓.

Go, wander in Minecraft and ⎓╎リ↸ ⎓𝙹∷ ᒲᒷ ℸ⍑╎ᓭ ᒷ̇/ᓵᒷ!¡ℸ╎𝙹リᔑꖎ ʖᒷ╎リ⊣.

Maybe you hoped to uncover the truth by skipping the trials and coming directly here? Not so fast. First you must solve the riddles of the Endercube in order to decipher the encrypted parts of this text. . . .

SOLUTIONS

NOVICE

THE EXPLORATION TRIAL

#1: (4) The volcano biome does not exist.

#2: The compass is missing.

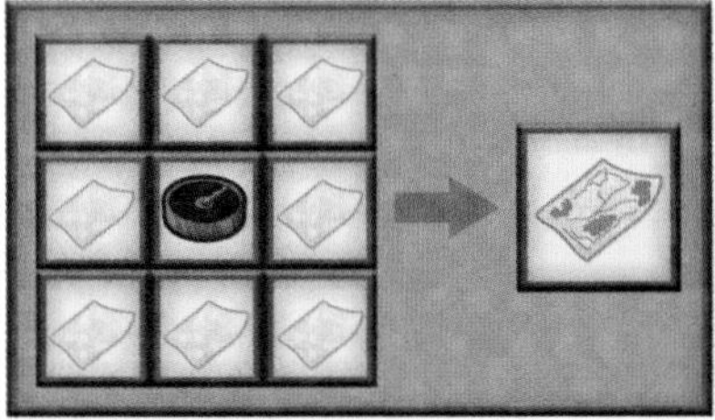

#3: (2) A boat can contain two characters.

#4: It's the sun. Look at the sky from time to time to see where the sun rises and sets—it's an excellent indicator!

#5: It's the cactus block. You can only find it in desert biomes.

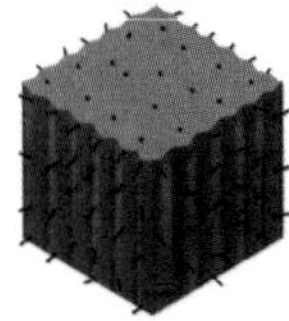

#6: There is only one wood block. You will need much more than that to face the dangers ahead!

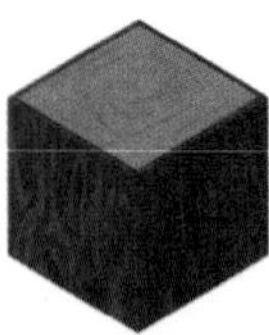

#7: (1) Temples are found in the jungle.

#8: (3) / (1) / (2) The horse is the fastest means of transportation, followed by the boat and the pig.

#9: The sun and the moon are hidden when it rains.

#10: (2) If you move too close to a polar bear while its cub is nearby, you will certainly regret it.

#11: (1) Given your skills, she could kill you with one look. A witch is very dangerous. You'd better leave her alone for now. As for setting the trees on fire . . . are you crazy?

#12: (2) A librarian. If you don't know that, it means you don't read enough books!

#13:

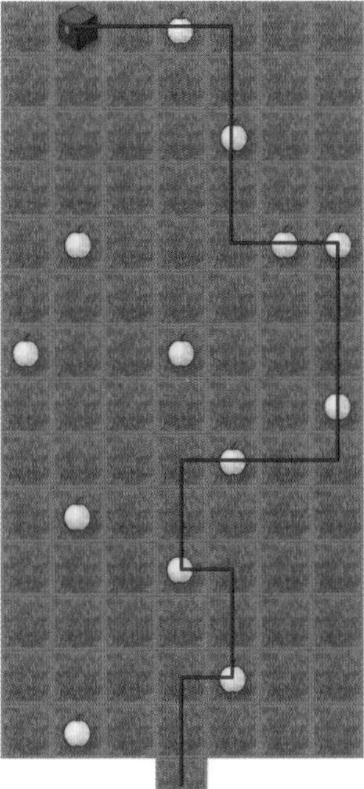

#14: (2) By placing a torch underwater at the same level as your head, you'll become a true amphibian.

#15: (1) A creeper explosion . . . what a sight to behold!

THE BUILDING TRIAL

#1: (1) Nothing beats a sturdy door to keep those miserable villagers alive!

#2: (1) The cactus. Be careful—it can sting very badly!

#3: It's the stone slab.

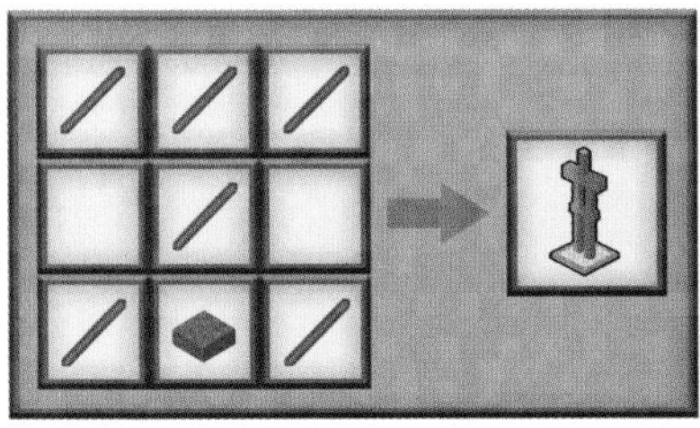

#4: (1) / (4) / (2) / (3)

#5: (2) It can carry redstone signals beyond fifteen blocks.

#6: (1) One furnace, one crafting table, and one chest. That should prove useful when you hear the monsters growl.

#7:

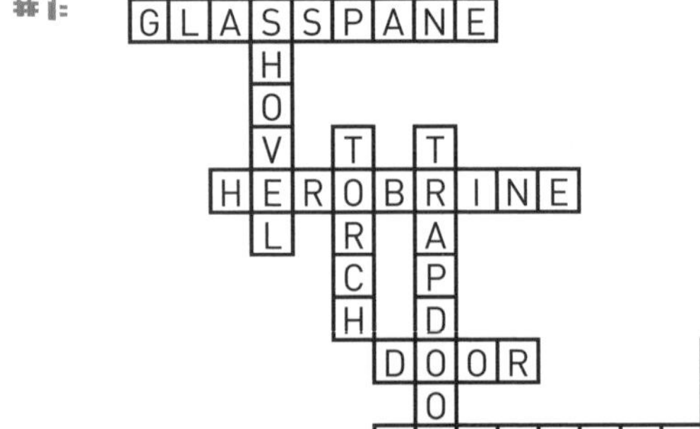

#8: You need a roof to protect Snowkin from the rain.

#9: (1) Monsters can't spawn on dirt roads, so feel free to build some around your house.

#10: (4) / (1) / (2) / (3)

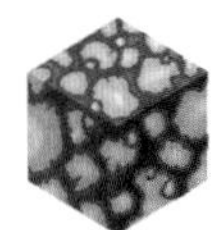   

#11: It's quartz.

#12: (1) Spiders are aggressive in battle, but unfortunately they're not all that smart. . . .

#13: (1)

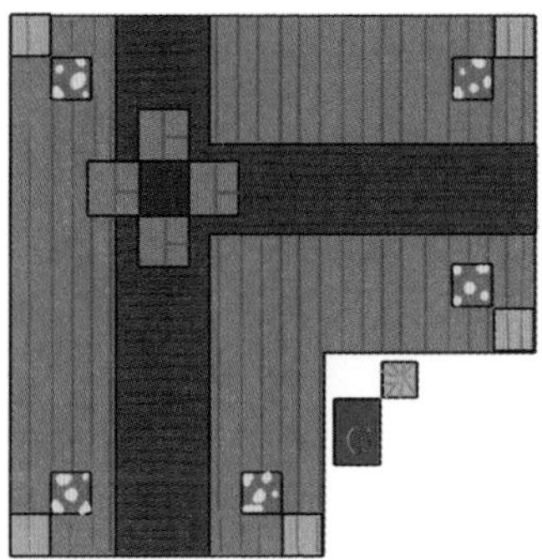

#14: (3) There are six types of wood.

#15: (4) / (2) / (1) / (3) / (5) / (6)

THE FARMING TRIAL

#1:

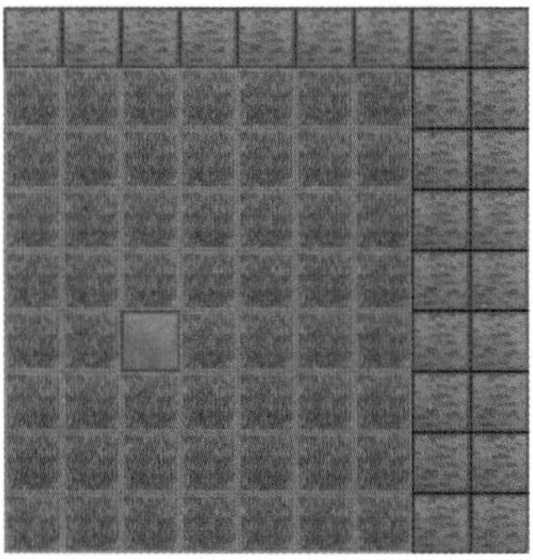

#2: (4), (6), and (8) Corn, pear, and strawberry do not exist in the game.

#3:

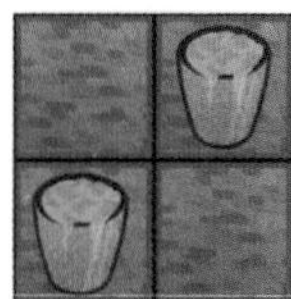

#4: A string is missing.

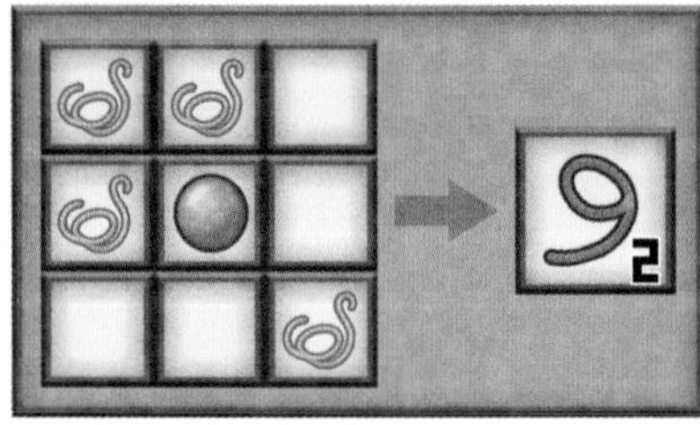

#5: (1): B. (2): A. (3): C. (4): D.

#6: (1) In villages.

#7: (2) A bucket of milk.

#8: Nine pumpkins.

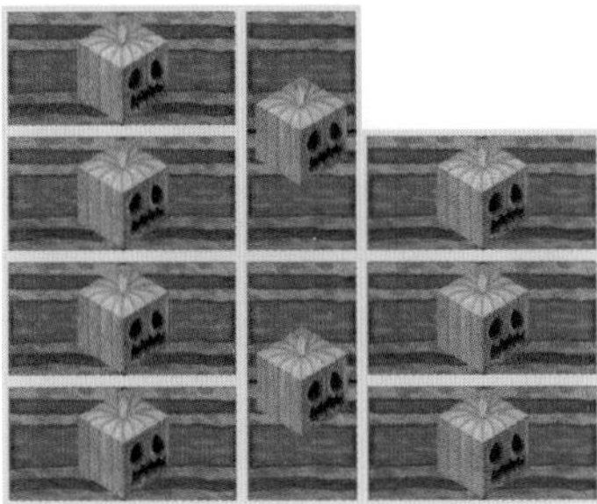

#9: (2) Nine llamas.

#10: (4) Allium.

#11: (2) Bone meal.

#12: (2) With an axe.

#13: Sugar cane cannot grow taller than three blocks.

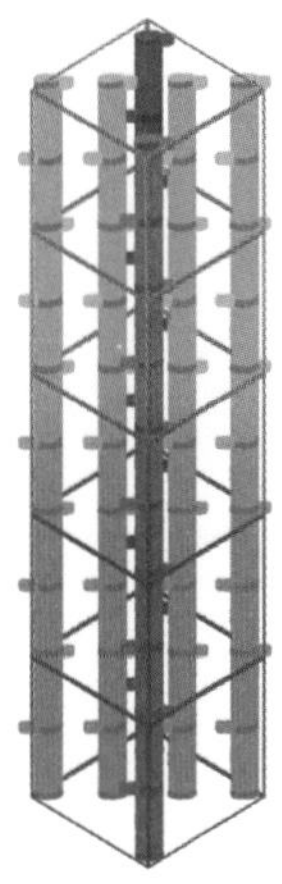

#14: (3) Six blocks.

#15: (2) They will fall in love.

THE MINING TRIAL

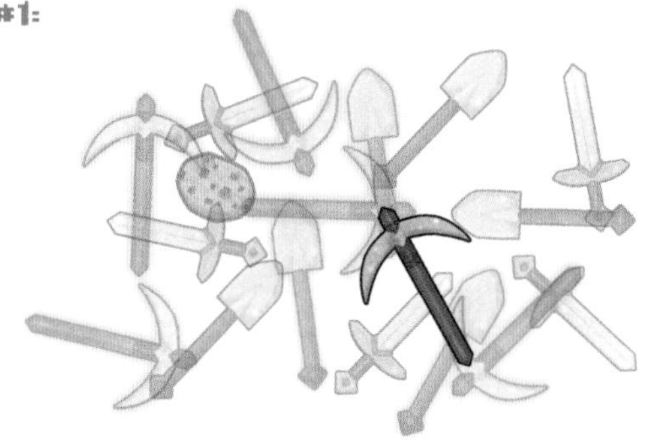

#2: (1) An iron pickaxe.

#3: (1) The bedrock.

#4: (2) Put a torch at the base of the column. An amazing technique!

#5:

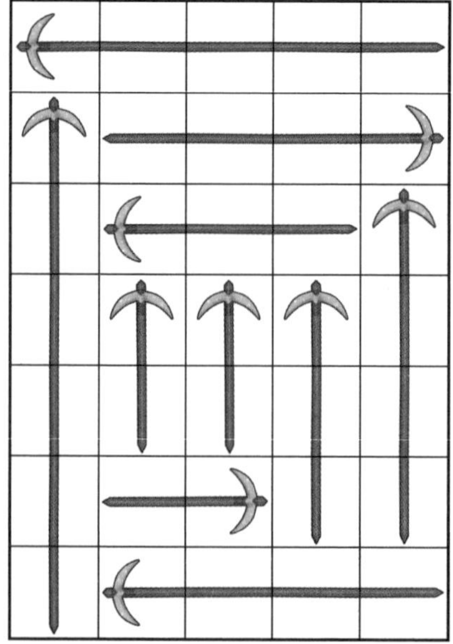

#6: (2), (6), and (8) Pumpkin, ice, and soul sand.

#7: (2) To dye terracotta in blue.

#8: (2) Emerald.

#9: (1) and (2) Chests and cave spider spawners.

#10: It's the stick.

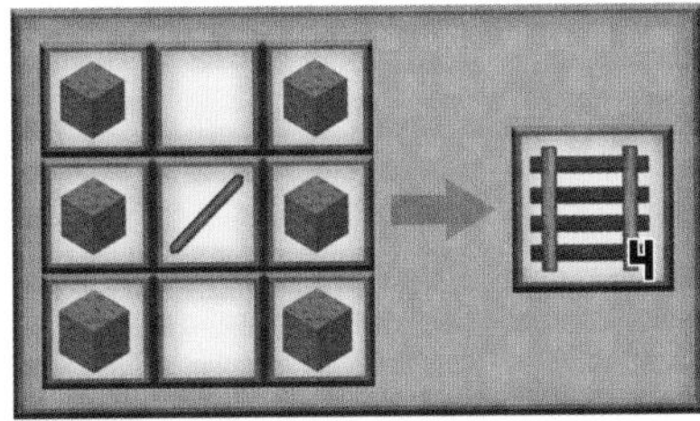

#11: (1) By killing a witch. Go easy on those poor women!

#12: Four stairs.

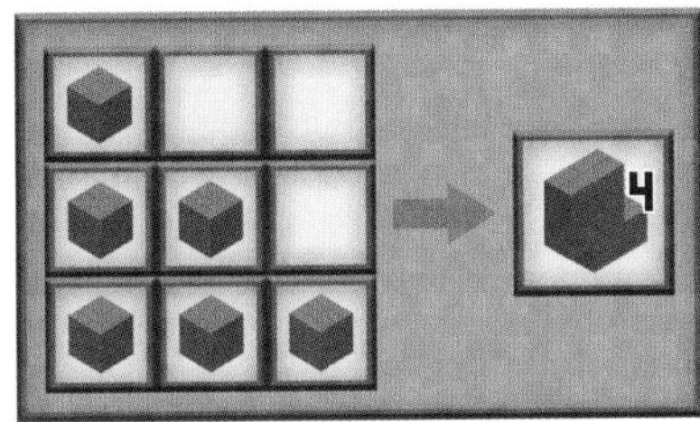

#13: (2) The minecart with glowstone.

#14:

#15: (3) Two shovels and two swords.

THE COMBAT TRIAL

#1: It's a block of wood planks.

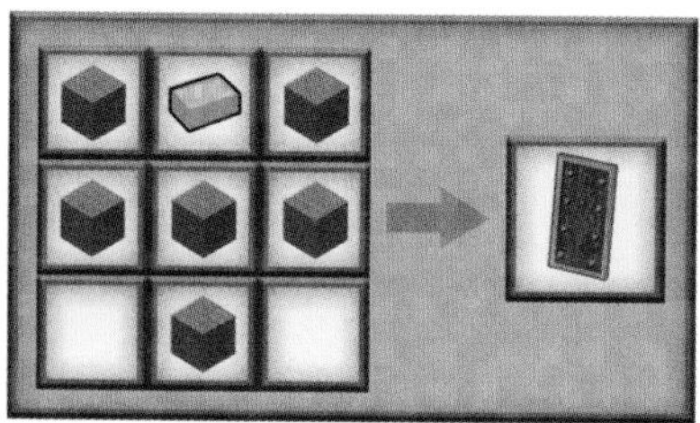

#2: (2) and (3) The zombie pigman and the ghast.

#3: (2) Repair uses the main material of a weapon, for instance, diamond.

#4: (2)

#5: (1) An exploding failed pig model! But where'd he get that idea in the first place?

#6: (2) Water and rain.

#7: (2), (3), (5), and (6) Creepers, spiders, slimes, and witches.

#8:

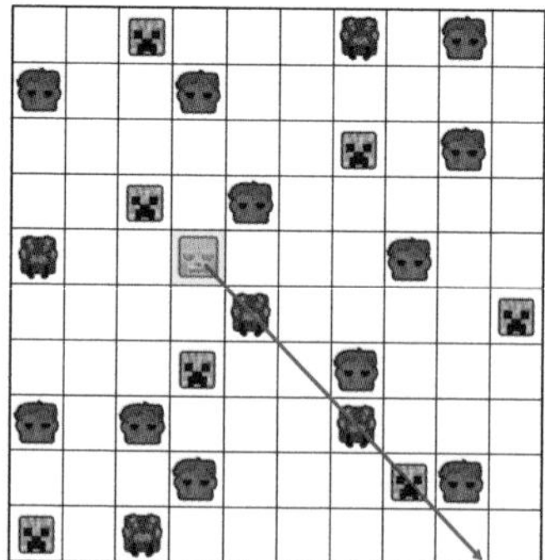

#9: (2) / (4) / (3) / (1)

#10: It's a vindicator.

#11: (2) One sword, one iron chestplate, and one pair of iron boots.

#12: (3) They do not take any damage when exposed to the sun.

#13: (3) A vial of potion.

#14: (1) Dogs.

#15:

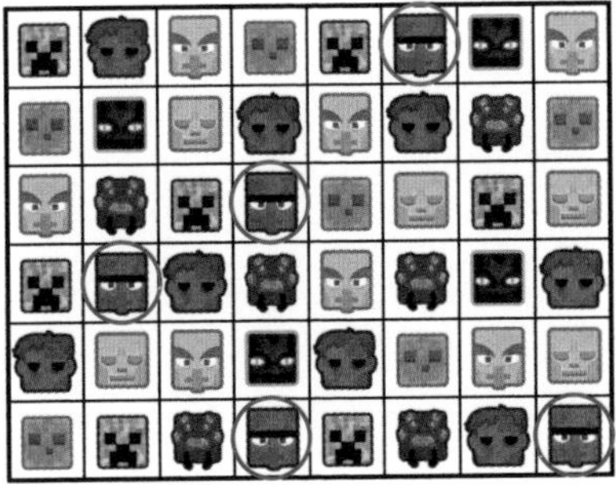

ENDERCUBE PUZZLE #1

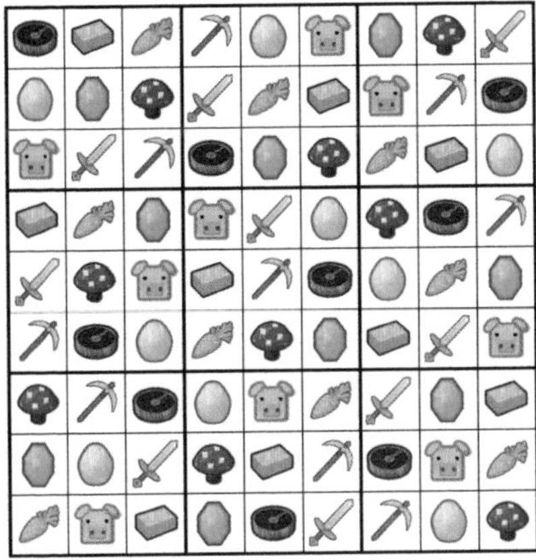

INITIATE

THE EXPLORATION TRIAL

#1: The map itself.

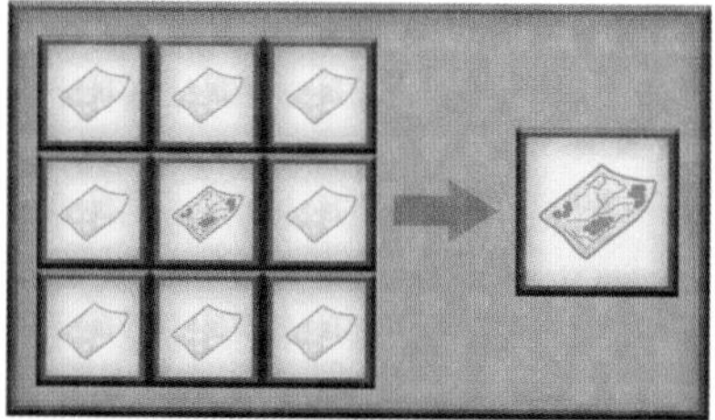

#2: (3) All zombie pigmen in the area will attack you.

#3: (2) There are no night-day cycles in the Nether, so it's important to avoid a temporal shift.

#4: (1) If a ghast fires on the portal, it will be deactivated and you won't be able to come back to the Overworld. You will thus need some flint and steel to reactivate it.

#5: (7) and (8) Granite and netherrack blocks.

#6: (3) A ghast spawner room.

#7: (2) When you move forward one block in the Nether, it corresponds to eight blocks in the Overworld.

#8: (1) Nothing at all; neither the occupant nor the minecart will cross the Nether portal.

#9: It's the redstone, the bucket of water, and the compass.

#10: (2) Some events are paused in the Overworld (weather, explosions, etc.).

#11: (1), (2), (3), and (4) All these monsters have a chance (or a risk, in your case) of crossing the Nether portal.

#12: (1) It slows you down as well as all other creatures.

#13: It's water.

#14: (3) In the upper left corner of the block, there is a pixelated "L." It will always point northward.

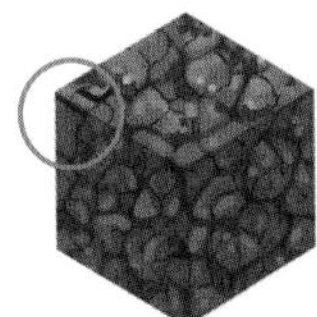

#15:

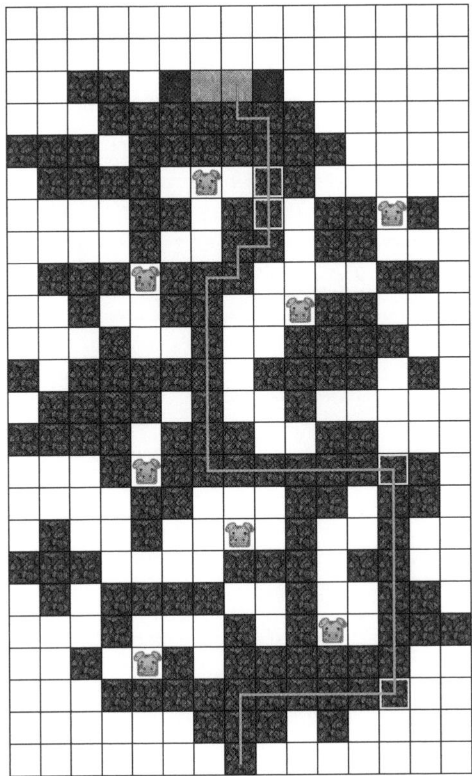

THE BUILDING TRIAL

#1: (1) A separation chamber is essential in case some monsters cross the portal.

#2: (3) The shelf.

#3: A stone block and a blaze rod.

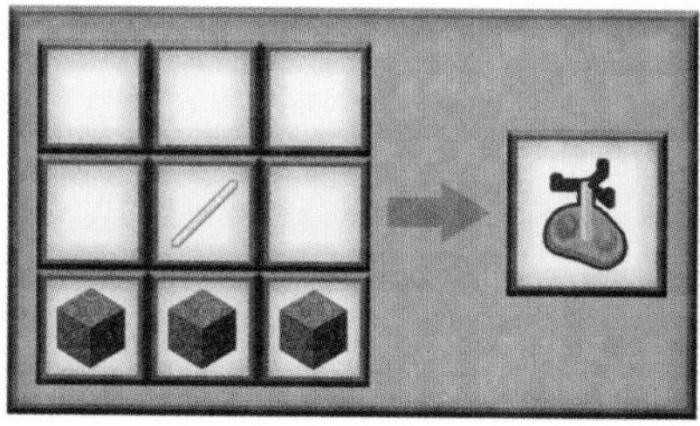

#4: (3), (5), and (6) These elements are either power transmission components or mechanical components interacting with redstone.

#5: One leather and two papers are missing.

#6: (1) He moves slowly, can't open doors, and spawns naturally in villages.

#7:
(1) and (8)
(2) and (6)
(3) and (7)
(4) and (12)
(5) and (11)
(9) and (10)

#8: (1) A block is only seven-eighths of the normal block height.

#9: (3) Fifteen bookshelves are required to maximize the power of an enchanting table.

#10: (1) A glass block.

#11: It's glowstone.

#12: (3) The TNT block will be placed in front of the dispenser, primed for explosion.

#13: (4) Hamburger.

#14: (1) The anvil does not move. (2) The packed ice is transformed. (3) The bed is destroyed. (4) The furnace does not move. (5) The jack o'lantern is destroyed. (6) The melon is transformed.

#15: (3) "The object displayed in the frame can be rotated six times" is wrong. The correct number is eight.

THE FARMING TRIAL

#1: (2) With a cauldron.

#2: (1) The warts must be placed on a block of soul sand.

#3:

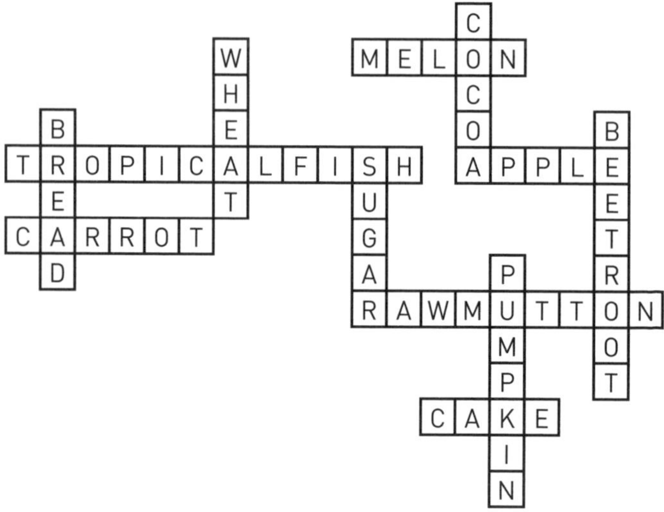

#4: (3) Glowstone can illuminate your crops so they keep growing at night.

#5: (2) Rabbit stew.

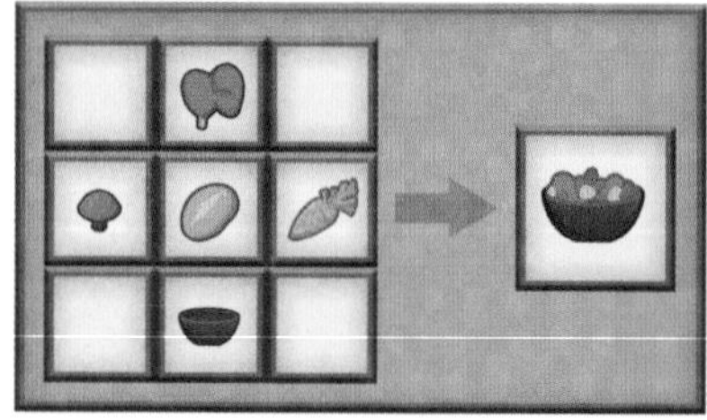

#6: (3) Your hunger level starts to drop.

#7: (1) The wolves must be at full health to fall in love.

#8: There is a barrier missing around the crops.

#9: (1) You can shave mushroom cows and milk them with a wooden bowl.

#10: (1) It reduces the wait time between two catches.

#11: (4) Cooked pork chop is the best food to satisfy your hunger.

#12: (1): A or C. (2): E. (3): A or C. (4): B. (5): D.

#13:

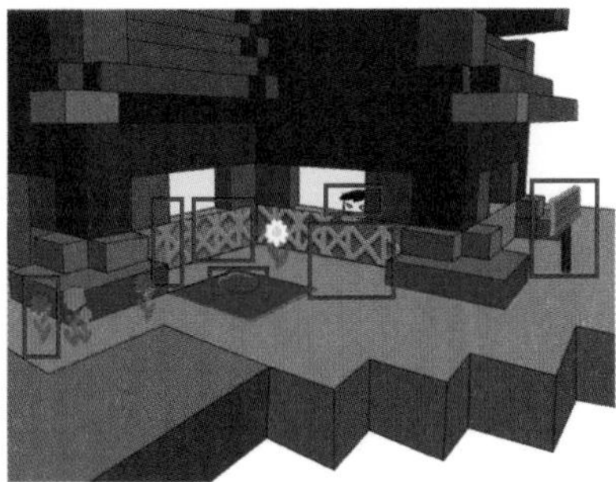

#14: (3) Raw chicken.

#15: (2) Flowers will grow in a seven-block radius.

THE MINING TRIAL

#1: (3) Two-thirds of the cauldron.

#2: Enchanting with an enchanting table consumes lapis lazuli blocks.

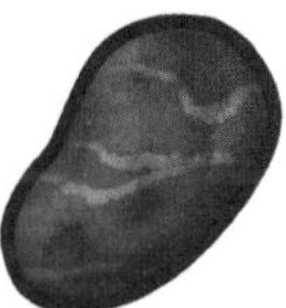

#3: (3) Two times faster than normal.

#4: (1), (2), and (4) Ice, glowstone, and iron ore.

#5: (1) Netherrack.

#6:

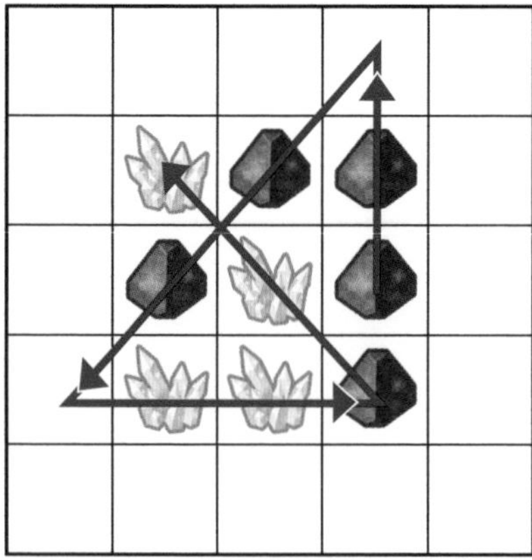

#7: (2) and (4) Sharpness and Looting.

#8: (1) Quartz is pretty common, like iron ore.

#9: (1) and (4) By killing a zombie and trading with a villager.

#10:

#11: (2) It's covered in moss. For a long time, it was thought to be blood. In fact, that stone was even nicknamed "bloodstone."

#12: It's furnace 2: Sixteen gold blocks and nine planks. Wood is not an efficient fuel; it burns too quickly.

#13: (2) Four minutes and ten seconds.

#14: Seven iron ingots, two sticks, and two gold ingots are missing.

#15: (3) You need a tunnel covering the whole railway. Otherwise, a ghast could launch a fireball at you and destroy your railroad.

THE COMBAT TRIAL

#1: (2), (3), and (5) The creeper, the enderman, and the slime.

#2: (1) A bow with the Flame enchantment.

#3: (2) A potion of Fire Resistance.

#4: (2) You need to grab them with a fishing rod.

#5: (1): D. (2): B. (3): C. (4): A. (5): E.

#6: (3) You most certainly will receive damage over time and die!

#7:

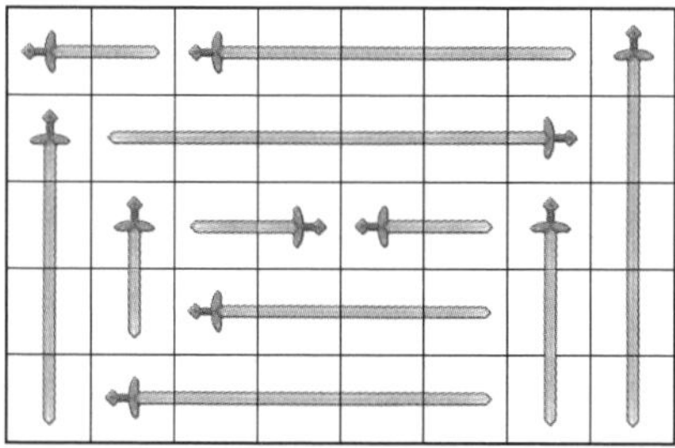

#8: (2) and (5) Wither arrows and arrows of Paralysis.

#9: (2) When a ghast goes through a lava fall, its speed decreases and it's immobilized for a few seconds.

#10: (3) Five.

#11: (1) An oxeye daisy.

#12: Three soul sand blocks and three wither skeletons heads.

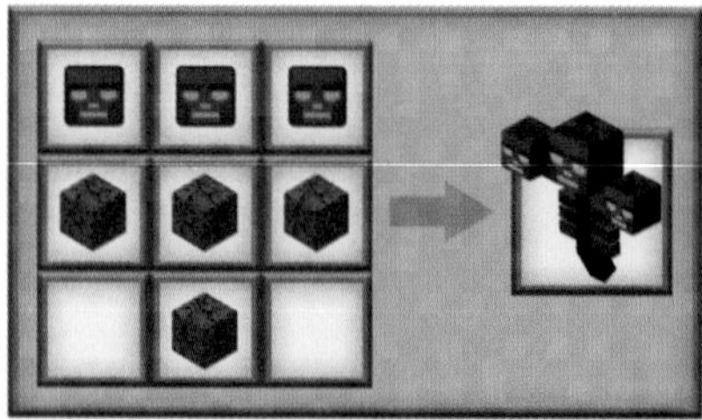

#13: (1) Withers are impervious to fire and lava, they will attack any creature except the undead, and their projectiles explode.

#14: A blaze.

#15: (1) Given the situation, only an ender pearl could save you, as you could teleport back at the top of the cliff.

ENDERCUBE PUZZLE #2

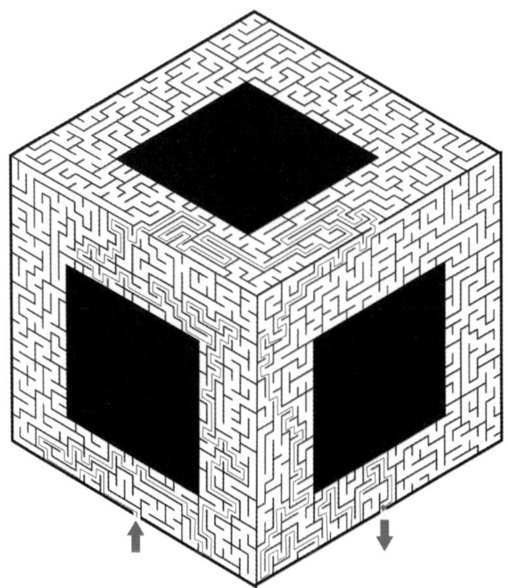

EXPERT

THE EXPLORATION TRIAL

#1: Some blaze powder is missing.

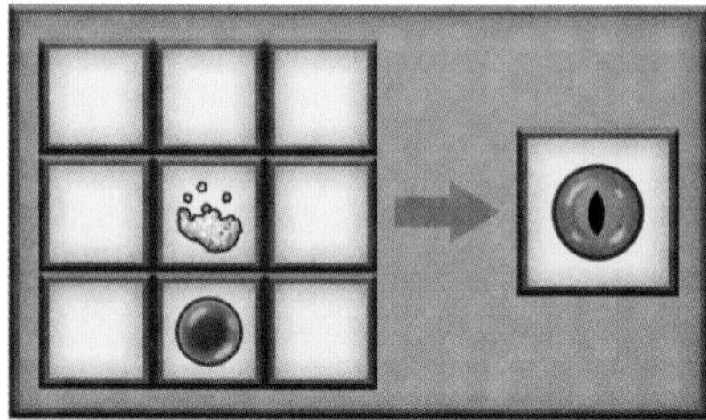

#2: (3) You need twelve eyes of ender to activate the portal.

#3: (2) You have to throw an eye of ender in the air; it will point the way.

#4: (1) Once across the portal, you appear on a floating section of obsidian.

#5: (4), (6), (7), (8), (9), (10), (11), and (12) It's the lava block, the soul sand block, the shulker box, the glowstone block, and the water, magma, dirt, and stone blocks.

#6: (1) A pumpkin will allow you to look at an enderman without being attacked. It's very useful, but your field of vision will be severely reduced.

#7: (2) It will display a map in gray and white.

#8: (1) and (2) It is much more resistant to explosions than normal stone and cannot be destroyed by the ender dragon.

#9: (2) You have to throw an ender pearl through the portal.

#10: (1.) A: Location of the dragon battle. B: Area likely to contain End cities. C: The limits of the End. D: Area likely to contain chorus trees.

#11: (1) In the End ship.

#12: (3) With the elytra, you can travel thirteen thousand blocks.

#13: (1) You need to push it with a piston block.

#14: It's an End crystal.

#15:

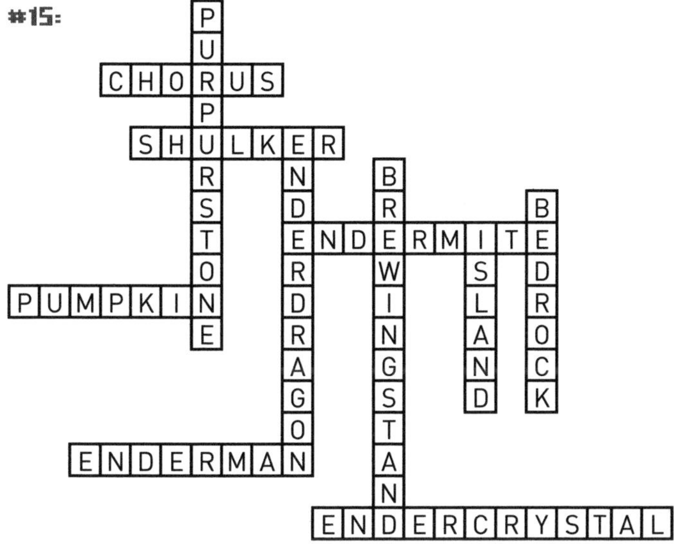

THE BUILDING TRIAL

#1: Five obsidian blocks and one eye of ender are missing.

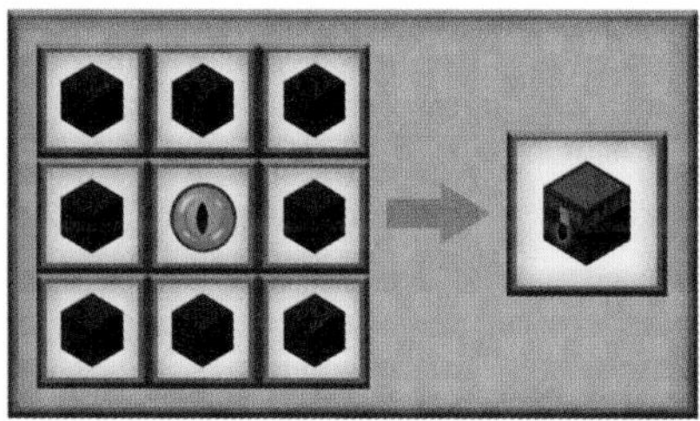

#2: (2) The ender chest is impervious to explosions.

#3: It's popped chorus fruit.

#4: (1) You can get a disc when a creeper is killed by a skeleton's arrow.

#5: (4) and (5) A block of End stone and a block of pink wool.

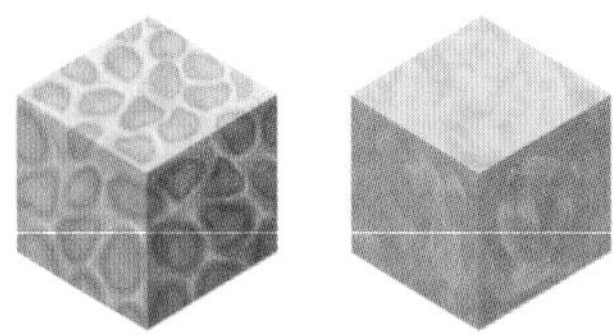

#6: Two shulker shells are missing. (2) The shulker box preserves its content when it's broken.

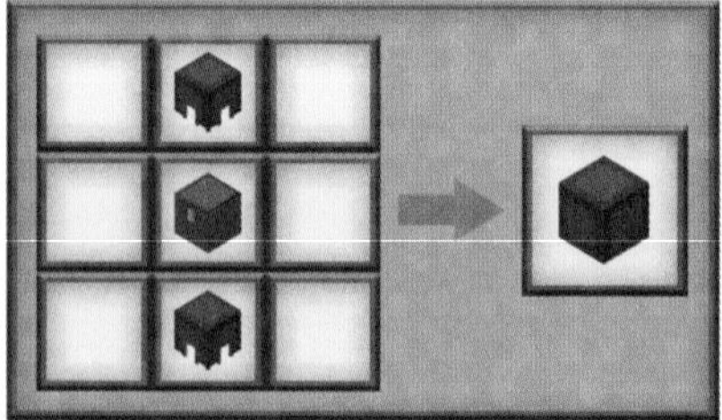

#7: Eight papers, one compass, twelve sticks, two stone slabs, one cooked rabbit, one brown or red mushroom, one cooked potato, one carrot, and one bowl.

#8: (2) Chiseled stone, chiseled purpur block, and chiseled quartz.

#9: (3) A beacon.

#10: (4) A torch.

#11: (1) The beacon projects a light beam skyward, visible from far away, and provides status effects to the player.

#12: (3) It creates an infinite loop of combusting and extinguishing.

#13: You just need to use a normal chest and a trapped chest.

#14: (1): A. (2): H. (3): C. (4): F. (5): G. (6): D. (7): B. (8): E.

#15: (2) The ender dragon will be revived.

THE FARMING TRIAL

#1:

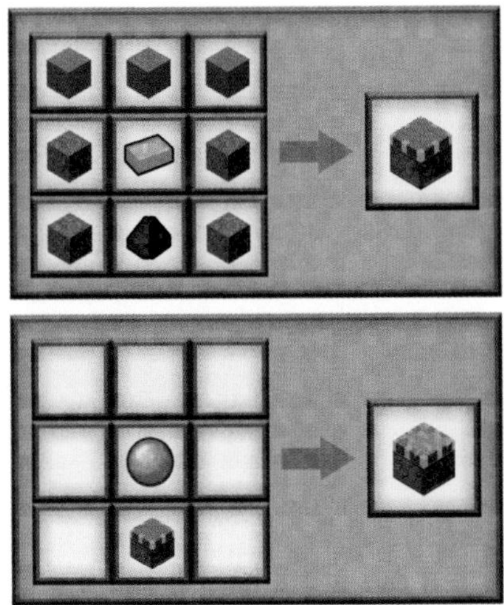

#2: (1) The mushroom island.

#3: (2) You have to stay a few blocks away from the ocelot, wait for it to come and ask for food, give it fish, and repeat until it's tamed.

#4: (3) It will try to sit on blocks, like furnaces, preventing you from using them.

#5: (1): C. (2): D. (3): A. (4): B. (5): E.

#6: (3) Animals killed with this weapon will drop cooked meat.

#7: See the image on the opposite page.

#8: (2) All of the other blocks of the plant will be destroyed.

#9: (2) You're teleported like an enderman, and then purple sparks fly around you.

#10: (3) Eight cookies.

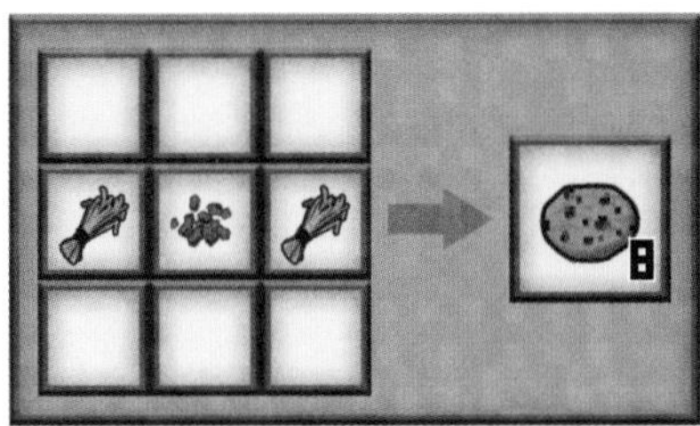

#11: (3) They need to grow vertically on jungle wood.

#12: (2) The plants will never grow.

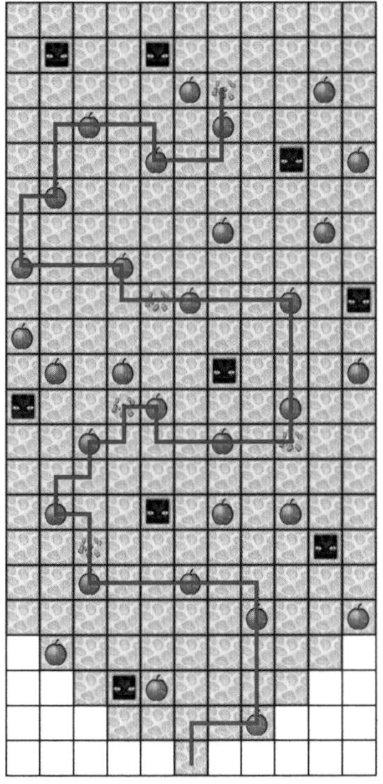

#13: It's the endermite.

#14: (1), (5), and (7) Cactus, Nether wart, and chorus plant.

#15: (3) Lightning strikes more often in the jungle biome, which can turn pigs into zombie pigmen.

Solution to **#7.**

THE MINING TRIAL

#1: (1): A. (2): C or F. (3): G. (4): E. (5): B or D. (6): B or D. (7): C or F.

#2: (3) In order to turn off a mob spawner, you must place torches everywhere in the dungeon and all around the spawner block. By placing torches on only the spawner itself, monsters still have a small chance of spawning.

#3: (2) Four diamonds.

#4: (2) Eight diamond ore blocks.

#5: Four iron ingots and one chest are missing.

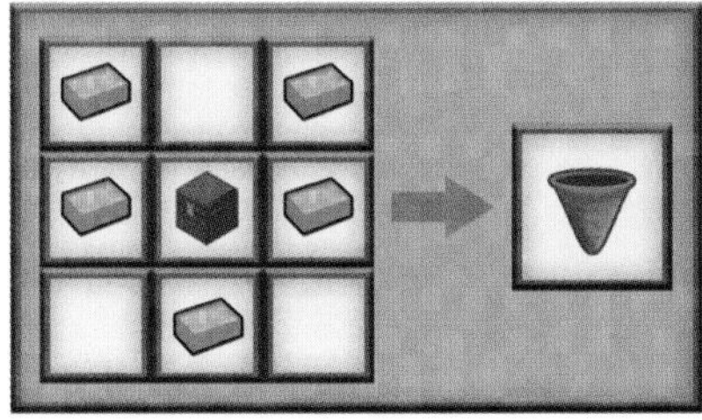

#6: (2) 30% faster than the previous level.

#7: (3) Nothing happens.

#8: (2) The TNT explosion is stronger than the creeper explosion.

#9: (2) and (3) A single repeater and a damage potion.

#10: (1) One diamond pickaxe, two chests, twelve ladders, one TNT, one minecart with hopper, and eight stairs.

#11: (3) You can easily destroy the block by hand.

#12:

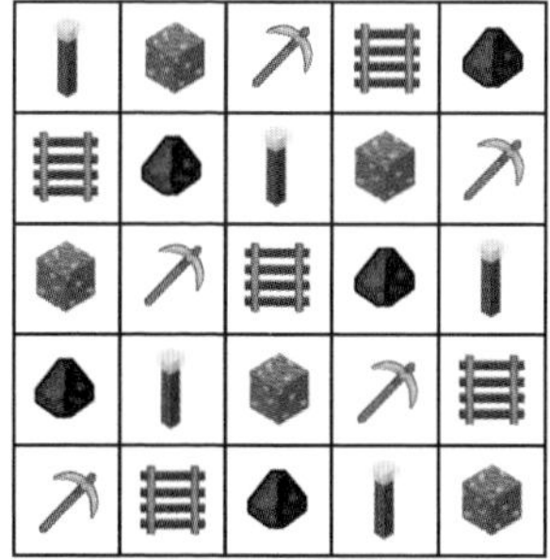

#13: (3) Sixty-four blocks away.

#14: (1) A golden carrot.

#15: (3) The minecart won't be able to go down the slope, but it will be able to go up it.

THE COMBAT TRIAL

#1:

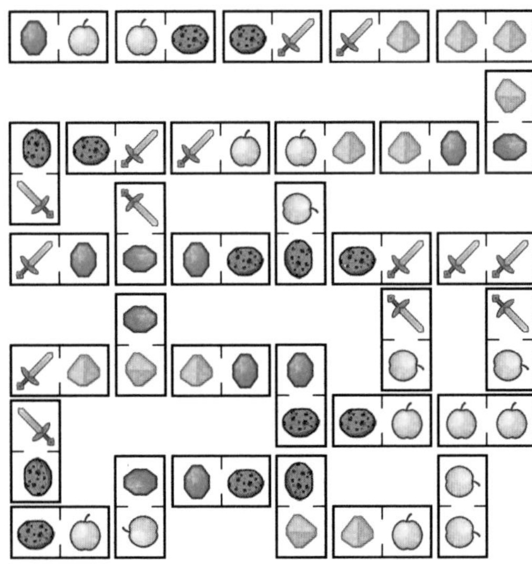

#2: (1) It will become hostile toward the dragon.

#3: (2) It will deal damage to the dragon.

#4: (1), (3), and (6) A snowball, a bow, and an egg.

#5: (3) The second- and third-smallest pillars.

#6: (2) The resulting explosion may hurt you.

#7: (2) The potion will become a lingering potion.

#8: (2) and (5) Falling on you to inflict area-of-effect damage and hitting you with her tail.

#9: (2) None. Death is inevitable.

#10: (2) Once equipped, the item can't be removed unless you die.

#11: (1): J. (2): D. (3): H. (4): G. (5): E. (6): A.

#12: (2) Their projectiles inflict the Levitation effect.

#13: (3) It teleports.

#14: (1) A bow.

#15:

Monster	Favorite animal	Favorite block	Age
Creeper	Pig	Gold block	8
Slime	Bear	Wood block	6
Zombie	Sheep	Obsidian block	7
Enderman	Cow	Diamond block	5

ENDERCUBE PUZZLE #3

A	ᔑ
B	ʖ
C	ᓵ
D	↸
E	ᒷ
F	⎓
G	⊣
H	⍑
I	╎
J	⋮
K	ꖌ
L	ꖎ
M	ᒲ

N	リ
O	𝙹
P	!¡
Q	ᑑ
R	∷
S	ᓭ
T	ℸ
U	⚍
V	⍊
W	∴
X	̇/
Y	||
Z	⨅

ENDERCUBE PUZZLE #3

CODE

IN LINES I
AM WRITTEN
WHEN I AM RED
PEOPLE PANIC
TO THE SOURCE
I AM LINKED

AGENT

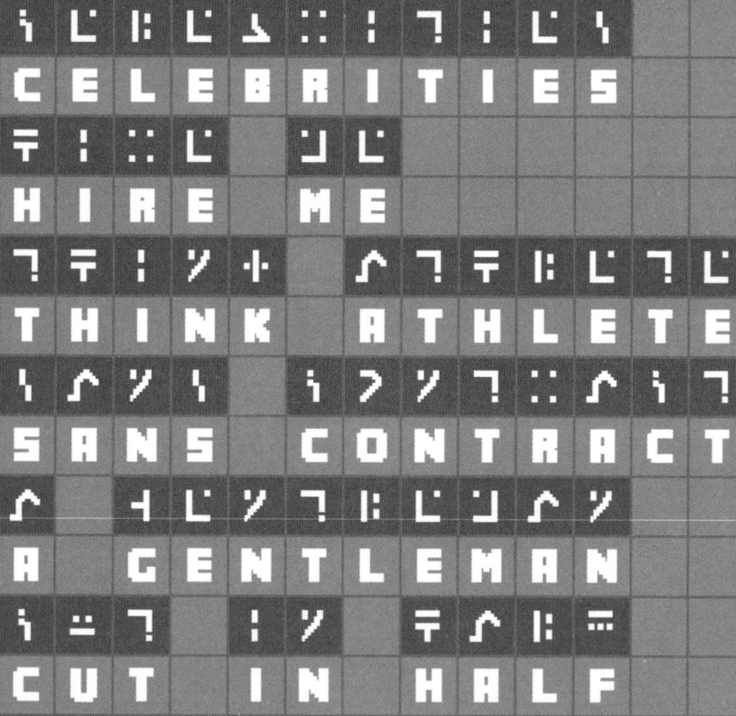
CELEBRITIES
HIRE ME
THINK ATHLETE
SANS CONTRACT
A GENTLEMAN
CUT IN HALF

ENDERCUBE PUZZLE #3

WEAPON

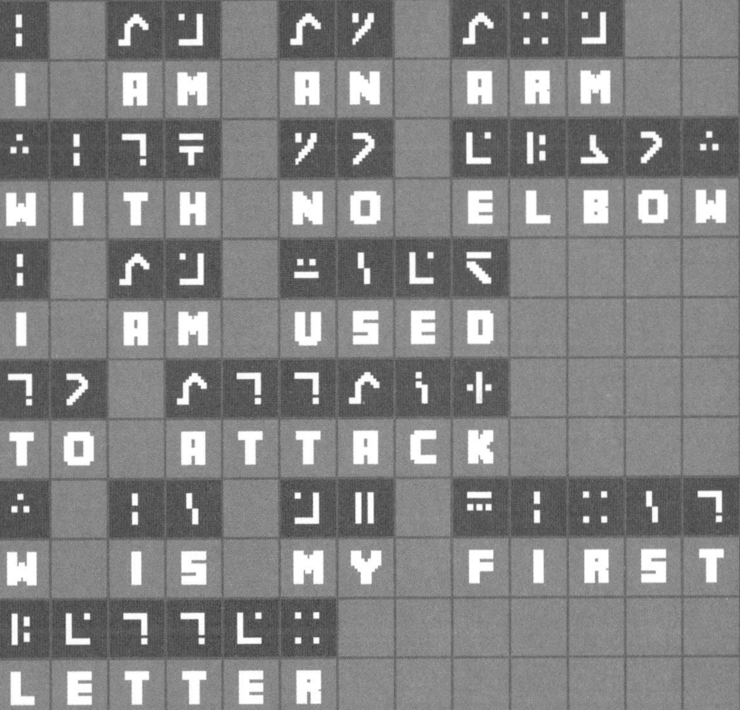

TOP

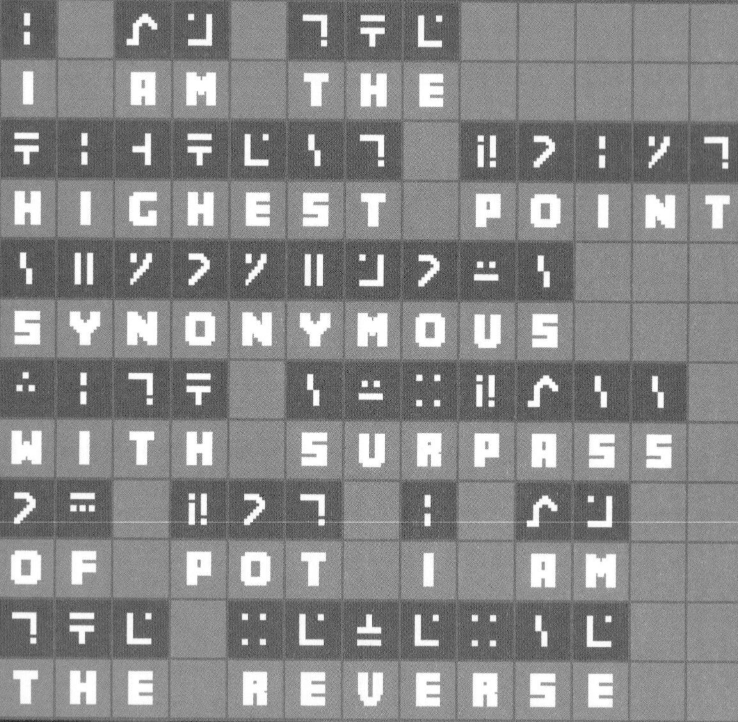
I AM THE
HIGHEST POINT
SYNONYMOUS
WITH SURPASS
OF POT I AM
THE REVERSE

ENDERCUBE PUZZLE #3

The password to open the Endercube is:

SECRET

ACKNOWLEDGMENTS

I'd like to thank Mathilde Auriac, without whom the Endercube would have never been possible. Her sketches and her support brought this dreadful relic to life, as well as this book. May the Master Crafters of Minecraft watch over you and guide you. Thanks also to Sébastien, Bleuenn, Fabrice, Julien, Claire, Piéric, and Noëmie, who helped make this project possible and have accompanied me through the different stages of its development. May you never fear the explosions of creepers.

ABOUT THE AUTHOR

Alain T. Puysségur was born in 1991 outside of Paris, France. At a very young age, he discovered authors like J. R. R. Tolkien, Robin Hobb, and J. K. Rowling—while also falling in love with the magic of video games and film. In the midst of these incredible and fantastic worlds, he dreamt of one day becoming a writer and inventing stories of his own. He now works as an author and game designer, giving life to every character he creates.

CHECK OUT THESE BOOKS FOR MORE UNOFFICIAL MINECRAFT ADVENTURES!